Come to Worship

COME TO WORSHIP

ROGER LOVETTE

BROADMAN PRESS
Nashville, Tennessee

© Copyright 1990 . Broadman Press
All rights reserved
4223-12
ISBN: 0-8054-2321-4
Dewey Decimal Classification: 264
Subject Heading: PUBLIC WORSHIP
Library of Congress Catalog Card Number: 89-37399
Printed in the United States of America

Unless otherwise stated, all Scripture quotations are from the *Revised Standard Version of the Bible,* copyrighted 1946, 1952, © 1971, 1973.
Scripture quotations marked KJV are from the King James Version of the Bible.
Scripture quotations marked Phillips are reprinted with permission of MacMillan Publishing Co., Inc. from J. B. Phillips: *The New Testament in Modern English,* Revised Edition. ©J. B. Phillips 1958, 1960, 1972.

Library of Congress Cataloging-in-Publication Data
Lovette, Roger, 1935-
    Come to worship / Roger Lovette
    p. cm.
    Includes bibliographical references.
    ISBN 0-8054-2321-4 :
    1. Public worship. I. Title.
BV15.L68 1990
264'.061--dc20

                                                89-37399
                                                CIP

To the saints of the First Baptist Church
Clemson, South Carolina
1975-1988
They let it happen.

CONTENTS

Introduction

Why do they come? Mrs. Jones in her mink. The old deaf man with the cane who will probably not hear a word. Why does that young man tag along with the girl? Why do the little ones, with their pencils and Sunday School papers, come back Sunday after Sunday? And why do those men with their smiles and pressed suits stand at the door with their bulletins week after week?

Some, of course, come out of habit. Some, bored by a week of dullness, come hoping to break the monotony of their barren lives. Some come to hold hands, while others come because their parents insist. Surely these reasons alone cannot explain why so many keep coming back week after week.

I think they come to worship. They come with some deep longing in their hearts to hear a word they have not heard before. Some come to receive comfort or find their sins forgiven. Others are there to discover an answer for the pressures that keep coming like the waves of the sea. They come to worship. To see, in their own way and in their own time, what Isaiah saw once upon a time when he looked up through blinding tears and a broken heart. To see, above the heartaches and headlines of too much, the Lord God Almighty. To know, despite what they have done and not done, that they are loved and cared for. That they count.

So I write this book for all those worship leaders who must sit down at the beginning of the week and try to address the hungers and hurts of those who will be there the next Sunday morning at 11 o'clock.

As I plan, week after week, I am haunted by a story that I read one summer when I was a seminary student. In *Clock Without Hands*, J.T. Malone is dying of leukemia. His life is a clock without hands. He knows the hour will strike but he does not know when. And so, in his desperation, knowing that he will soon die, he goes to church.

> Afraid to talk to the doctors, unable to speak of anything intimate with his own wife, Malone just blundered silently. Every Sunday he went to church, but Dr. Watson was a folksy preacher who spoke to the living and not to a man who was going to die. He compared the Holy Sacraments with a car. Saying that people had to be tanked up once in a while in order to proceed with their spiritual life. This service offended Malone, although he did not know why. The First Baptist Church was the largest church in town with property worth, offhand, two million dollars. The deacons were men of substance. Pillars of the church, millionaires, rich doctors, owners of utility companies. But though Malone went every Sunday to church, and though they were holy men, in his judgment, he felt strangely apart from them. Though he shook hands with Dr. Watson at the end of every church service, he felt no communication with him, or any of the other worshippers.[1]

J.T. Malone sits at my elbow week after week. I keep asking, over and over again, will what we do next Sunday speak to his needs and to the needs of all the others that come?

In many ways the Evangelical Church faces a grave crisis. Recently someone, at a national worship conference, said that, "We don't know what worship is. And we don't know because our leaders don't know what worship is." This is scary. This scholar went on to say: "We don't know what worship is experientially or theologically. We have called anything and everything worship." He says: "We have so emphasized the human side of God's plan that we have humanized something very God-centered. God can't be first if the functions and actions that make Him first are second. Worship is about the priority of God in our values, affections and commitments."[2]

This book seeks to deal with the priorities of our worship. These words have been a long time in coming. In some ways I think I have been writing it for 27 years—the length of time I have served as a pastor. When I first began, in the early 1960s, there were few guides and helps for worship. We are better served now. But even today, after all these years, churches and ministers flounder when it comes to Sunday morning at 11 o'clock.

So this book is for beginning preachers who are wondering which way to go. This is a book for preachers on the run, who must sandwich in worship preparation and sermons between a multitude of other demands. This book is to help laypersons get a better handle on one of the most important occasions in the life of the local church. There are questions at the end of every chapter which I hope will be a springboard for deacons and other church leaders on retreat or in their monthly meetings. Worship leaders might use the chapter headings for Sunday night or Wednesday evening discussions. And it is my hope that ministers of music will find what is written here helpful.

This is a workbook to help you hammer out your own

concepts of worship. This is an idea book which might provide a springboard for you to help make worship in the place where you serve happen in a more meaningful way. This is a dream book that someone, reading these words, might catch the spirit of a church where praise and adoration become the most important thing they do. But most of all, I think, this is a hopeful book—that because of your own work where you are, someone, somewhere out there in the pews will see what Isaiah saw, years ago, and in the seeing they will never be the same again.

If, through these pages, someone decides to work a little harder at this business of worship, all these efforts will not have been in vain.

I could not have finished this task without that great cloud of witnesses in five churches that have let me be their pastor. Nor could I have written much at all without two great secretaries, Jean Thomas and Joyce Hawkins, and my colleagues in music ministry: Bill Vessels, Stewart Sharp, Bob Hill, Joel Reed, James Bennett, and Wayne Randolph. I am also indebted to James Bennett, Gayle Lovette, Wayne Randolph, John Wallace, and Randy Wright, for reading the manuscript and offering many helpful suggestions. But even more than these is that family of mine, Leslie, Matthew, and dear Gayle, who have shared with me through their trust and love more than they will ever know.

So let us begin. Hopefully this book will help you in the great adventure of seeing the Lord.

Notes

1. Carson McCullers, *Clock Without Hands* (New York: Bantam Books, 1963), 137-140.

2. Quoted in *Church Music Upbeat*, (Spring, 1988) published by the Church Music Department, The Sunday School Board of the Southern Baptist Convention, 2.

Prelude

It is eleven o'clock on Sunday morning. The setting varies, but the act is always the same. The church doors have been unlocked hours before. Someone has checked the heat or the air-conditioning. The ushers are in place with a smile and a bulletin. The organ or piano—sometimes both—play in the sanctuary. People—old and young—come from all over. Upstairs, somewhere, if you listen closely, you can hear a choir practicing. People nod to one another and smile. There is a hum of whispers across the room. Mrs. Jones looks around, hoping no one will notice. She just wants to know who's there. Her eye falls on a nice-looking young man with a girl she taught in Sunday School ten years before. An old man with a cane asks, in a loud voice, where the hearing stations are. Children, fresh from Sunday School, run to meet their parents. Then the choir files in and the preacher and the minister of music. The doors close. The whispering slowly dies down. The preacher steps to the pulpit and says: "Let us pray." Worship begins with heads bowed and hearts open in little towns and big cities all over the world.

1
Rock or Sand

First we shape our buildings, then our buildings
shape us.

—Winston Churchill

Every one then who hears these words of mine and
does them will be like a wise man who built his house
upon the rock; and the rains fell, and the floods
came, and the winds blew and beat upon that house,
but it did not fall, because it had been founded on the
rock. And every one who hears these words of mine
and does not do them will be like a foolish man who
built his house upon the sand; and the rain fell, and
the floods came, and the winds blew and beat against
that house, and it fell; and great was the fall of it
(Matt. 7:24-27).

When we come to worship, the Evangelical Church
stands at a crossroads. The opportunity we face is to confront mystery in such a way that God's voice is clearly
heard and understood. Many churches today find themselves subjected to the fads of our time, the biases of ministers and churches. Having *lethargy*, many seek to create
their own worship forms. The tragedy is that worship
may degenerate into mere entertainment, titillating the
emotions, giving the worshipers little of substance to live
by.

Some basic structure must be considered if corporate
worship is to stand against the strong winds that blow in

15

our time. So, form is as foundational for worship as it is to
architecture. Evangelicals discovered in their early days
that too much structure could be stifling. Later they came
to realize that too little structure produces uncertainty
and chaos.

C. S. Lewis once observed that, if the church must pay
too much attention to their feet, they cannot enjoy the
dance.[1] Churches today face the hard task of dealing with
a framework which can liberate and offer some vision of
God, yet at the same time never be so cumbersome that
the people lose the way.

What are some basic elements of structure that are in-
herent in every worship experience if worship is to help
the congregation experience the Lord?

Strong Biblical Base

George Adam Smith has said that we discover the secret of all Isaiah did when we turn to his call which is
recorded in Isaiah 6.[2] The prophet's whole ministry can
be traced back to that hard time when he limped into the
Temple and discovered his life changed forever.

Here we find as autobiographical a passage as we have
in the Bible. Here we discover a concrete definition of authentic worship. Isaiah "saw the Lord" and, in that seeing, his life was never the same. Worship, in the Old Testament, meant "to bow down or prostrate oneself." This
posture indicated a reverence or homage given to a lord,
whether human or divine. In the New Testament we find
this same definition of worship. The word meant primari-
ly to "bow down." Drawing from the Old Testament roots,
the word also meant service and piety.[3]

Biblical worship is rooted in reality.—"In the year that
King Uzziah died, I saw the Lord " (Isa. 6:1). No greater
king had come to Israel since King David. For fifty years
Uzziah had served his people well. National pride had
been restored. This king had held back the enemy. He had

made the kingdom proud once more. But then leprosy at-
tacked the king and after years of suffering he died. This
was the setting of Isaiah's great vision. His great encounter was rooted in the reality of a life knee-deep in a grief
for himself and his people. With the great Uzziah now
dead, Isaiah wondered what would happen to him and his
people.

There is no biblical worship that is not wedded to reality. Perhaps Karl Barth's definition of preaching says it
best, "We must stand with the Bible in one hand and the
daily newspaper in the other." No worship can strike to
the heart of life that is not rooted in the reality of its time.
Biblical worship is set in the context of the world where
the worshiper lives.

The Bible is filled with stories of people struggling with
the realities of faith in a hard time. Abraham and Sarah
seeking a country they did not know, Moses in Midian
and Egypt and that long wilderness journey. Prophet after prophet railed out against the disjointedness of their
lives and their time. Building on this solid base of reality,
the New Testament came into being. John the Baptist
would speak against Herod's sin and lose his life. Jesus'
timeless words were shaped by His time and place. And
Paul would crisscross his world with a message set down
in places like Corinth, Galatia, and Thessalonica. The
faith journey was hammered out in the cauldron of human experience.

Worship cannot escape the context of its time. And the
worship leader must give attention to the world in which
the worshipers live. "In the year that King Uzziah died..."
reminds us that the treasure comes in some earthen ves-
sel of the here and now. Ignore this context and the service becomes irrelevant, obtuse, ill-defined, and frag-
mented. "God so loved *the world* . . ." frames the church's
agenda every Sunday as it sings its hymns and offers its
prayers.

Worship is rooted in God.—When King Uzziah died,
Isaiah "saw the Lord sitting upon a throne, high and lifted up" (Isa. 6:1). Worship would be a poor thing if it was
only rooted in the reality of the present tense. But in the
middle of a terrible time, the prophet was given a vision
of God. This was the encounter that changed his life
forever.

Worship is only real and life-changing when we are
confronted with the mystery of the ages. Newspapers and
magazines give us reality enough. The media deals with
the everydayness of life. We need some moments when we
are transported beyond the mundane to a vision that will
transform the ordinary into the holy.

Unless our worship focuses chiefly on this seeing of God
we will have missed everything. This is the meeting, the
encounter, of which the Scriptures speak continually. For
this is the place where we take off our shoes knowing that
the ground on which we stand is more than ground, and
bread is more than bread. That which we begin to see
with eyes of faith is greater than the world we usually
inhabit.

Whatever happens in worship, there must be this transcendent vision of the Lord God Almighty high and lifted
up. If we miss this seeing, nothing that we do in church
really matters. Here Isaiah came to realize the holiness,
the otherness, and the sovereignty of God. This prophet's
new perceptivity gave the totality of life a shape it did not
have before his coming.

Worship is rooted in confession.—Isaiah's response to
all of this mystery, this smoke, this vision of glory and
wonder was to confess his sins. "Woe is me! For I am lost;
for I am a man of unclean lips, and I dwell in the midst of
a people of unclean lips" (Isa. 6:5). His eyes had seen the
King; and, in that new light, he witnessed the poverty of
his own life against the backdrop of a holy God.

Place these words down against so much in church today. This cult of feel-good, of whistle-while-you-work, nar-
row nationalism, and affirming whatever prejudices we
bring into the house is not found here. Each worshiper
should find some moment when he or she must look at
their lives the way they are and see themselves in the reality of the light of Almighty God.

Worship is rooted in forgiveness.—"Then flew one of
the seraphim to me, having in his hand a burning coal
which he had taken with tongs from the altar. And he
touched my mouth, and said: 'Behold, this has touched
your lips; your guilt is taken away, and your sin forgiv-
en' " (Isa. 6:6-7).

People complain that they often feel worse after church
than before they went. Some refuse to go back again because they do not like the feelings that the service engen-
ders in their lives. Such a service misses the heart of worship. Isaiah discovered that he was forgiven. All the
wrongs of his life were dealt with. He walked out of that
Temple turned inside out. Whatever else worship is to
do—it is to help the worshiper discover the forgiveness of
God.

Worship is rooted in response.—"And I heard the voice
of God saying, 'Whom shall I send, and who will go for us?'
Then I said, 'Here am I! Send me.' And he said, 'Go' " (Isa.
6:8-9). Many services of worship print at the end of their
ordered service:

The end of worship—
The beginning of service.

All worship is rooted in response. Response comes in
many ways, but the worshiper is to answer the good news
that comes. Sometimes it may mean a sin is forgiven,
sometimes it means that a new resolve is born, sometimes

it means to ask forgiveness of a brother or sister, sometimes it means to change one's life or begin again. Worship means that we *do* something.

In the New Testament the old sacrifices demanded in
the Old Testament have been scrapped. Since the death of
Jesus on Calvary, the believers discovered that the service he or she was to render was linked to the believer's
new experience and not some offering that would atone
for sin.[4] Years before the coming of Christ, Isaiah captured this dimension of worship. Here we find the beginning of his great call. In the Temple, in a hard time, he
saw the Lord—he heard a voice that confronted him with
the frailty and sin of his life. After he was forgiven he
responded by the giving of himself in service.

There will be little worship, despite the form, if the
church today does not return to a service rooted in reality, in God, and in discovering forgiveness and responding
to a call. This is the rocklike foundation Jesus dreamed of
when He called His disciples to follow Him. Alongside
this cornerstone of a strong biblical base we must give attention to a second foundation stone.

Strong Historical Base

Some time ago a minister moved to a new church. On a
visit to a large and impressive liturgical church, he was so
struck with their formal service of worship that, when he
returned home, he transposed that entire service into his
Sunday worship. The result was that his people revolted.
They hated the changes their new pastor had made. That
minister learned a painful lesson. You cannot use another's tradition as one's own—you must begin where the
people are.

The problem that so many have made in trying to reform their own worship is that they have tried to turn
their church's service into some sort of quasi-Presbyteri-
an or Episcopal worship. Everything is done in decency

and in order—but such revisions fail to reflect the historical base of the congregation. Worship reform will fail unless it is wed to a careful understanding of your own particular history.

My own particular history comes from a Baptist background. You would have to research the background of your own denomination in order to understand the historical base for your own particular worship style. Let me show you from my historical background how you learn from your own history.

Two strands form the evangelical base for our worship. Early Baptists tapped two tributaries that are still obvious to this day. Both strands need to be incorporated for worship to be tied to our tradition. The first strand comes from our English roots where Baptists first emerged. The second strand can be found in the frontier of the new land where Baptists finally moved. Steven Winward has called these tributaries liturgy and liberty. Woven together they form a solid tie with Baptists' historical roots. Those in favor of worship have opted either for the formal liturgical service or the freewheeling service of the frontier. We must give attention to both features if worship reflects our roots with the past. First we must look at our English beginnings, then we will examine the frontier tradition.

Baptist beginnings can be traced back to the 17th century where a little cluster of Separatists gathered to participate in illegal worship. The Anglicans forbade any worship that was not prescribed by the state church. These believers ignored the law. They met with no printed order of service, no hymnbooks, not even a copy of the Bible. The one binding tie which that fellowship determined to follow was the leadership of God as "the Lord's free people." Out of that yearning for freedom at least six principles emerged in early English worship patterns.

Openness to change and flexibility.—John Smyth and his followers reacted strongly to the rigid Anglican worship of their time. All worship was prescribed: prayers, sermons, Scriptures—everything was read. *The Book of Common Prayer* rigidly dictated the worship of that time.[5] Early Baptists, led by independent thinkers like Smyth, dared to break with prescribed worship knowing full well they were breaking the law.

This is what we find:

> We begynne wth a prayer, after reade some one or two chapters of the bible, gyve the sence thereof, and conferr vpon the same, that done wee lay aside oure bookes, and after a solemne prayer made by the .1. speaker, he propoundeth some text ovt of the scripture and prophesieth ovt of the same by the space of one hower, or the Quarters of an hower. After him standeth vp A.2.speaker and prophesieth ovt of the same text the like tyme and place sometyme more sometyme lesse. After him the .3. the .4. and .5. as the tyme will geve leave. Then the .1. speaker cocludeth wth prayer as he began wth prayer wth an exhortation to cotribution to the poore, wch collection being made is also cocluded with prayer. This morning exercize begynes at eight of the clock, and cotinueth vnto twelve of the clocke, the like course and exercise is observed in the afternoone from .2. of the clock vnto .5. and .6. of the clocke. last of all the execution of the govermet of the church is handled.[6]

The great gift which our forebears gave us was a willingness to experiment and to place our ordered worship down beside the Holy Scriptures. The church body whose worship patterns remain the same week after week and year after year needs to study early Baptist worship. They were determined that no order was sacred which did not allow the Spirit of God to flow freely into the life of the church. So we come to the second contribution that we find in early Baptist worship.

Openness to the Spirit.—For John Smyth the most important element in spiritual worship was to allow the Spirit of God to move among the worshipers. This is why he resisted, for a time, anything printed during the service. He wrote at length about the problem of "quenching the Spirit." Smyth pointed out that the Spirit could be quenched in two ways: 1) by silence or 2) by any set forms of worship.[7] Anything which might in any way be construed as hampering the Spirit of God was scrapped by those early believers.

Perhaps one of the reasons that the charismatic movement has grown so in the 20th century is because so many of our churches have become too ordered and predictable. Sameness dominates so much that we do. Only those congregations that are willing to risk change will be able to tap this second great gift of the early Baptist tradition: openness to the Spirit of God.

Freedom of conscience.—We must understand the context out of which Smyth and his followers worked. In that time freedom was suspect. The principle of freedom of conscience was all but eliminated from the church's life. So there arose a movement that reacted against prescribed authority. The Lord's free people were unwilling for any outside authority to impose belief or prescribed forms on them.[8]

The need for order.—But excesses usually follow renewal. This was certainly true in early Baptist life. They reacted so strongly to openness and freedom of conscience that often their services moved to the point of chaos and disorder.

Thomas McKibbens points out that in 1647 George Fox taught of the "inner light" and many Baptists began to join the newly found Quaker movement. Such dependence on the "inner light" produced havoc in the churches. Fox was so extreme that he even challenged the primacy of the Scriptures. There developed in Evangelical circles the need for order which was set in the context of freedom of conscience and a constant listening to the Spirit. Between 1673-1691 Benjamin Keach, a Baptist pastor, was advocating the composition of sermons, prayers, and hymns.[9]

So there developed a hunger for order. No set patterns were prescribed, but emphasis began to be placed on "things done with decency and order" while allowing great spontaneity from congregation to congregation. In studying early Baptist life, no place was this order more apparent than in the intense study that Baptist pastors gave to the preaching of the Word. So we move to the next gift the early Baptists have given us.

A tradition of great preaching.—If the 17th century was characterized by openness to the Spirit and freedom of conscience, there arose in the next century an emphasis on great preaching. Powerful preachers arose during this time which helped to shape the Baptist tradition to this day. John Rippon, John Ryland, Andrew Fuller, and William Carey were some of the early preachers that set the high standard for all that would follow.

People came to church to hear the Word of God preached in all its power. The churches flourished and grew as they found faithful interpreters of the Word of God. Those early sermons were characterized by a strong emphasis on the authority of the Scriptures.

Centrality of the Scriptures.—The Holy Scriptures became the standard by which all else would be judged. Preaching became central because it was grounded in the Word that came from the Lord. So Baptist worship came to be "a Service of the Word set in the context of prayer and praise."[10]

No real worship renewal can take place today without some understanding of biblical principles. The authority of the Word is foremost in understanding our early Baptist roots. Those pastors that aim for the high standard of worship will do well to return to the Holy Scriptures for understanding and direction for our troubled time.

These were the elements that Baptists brought to the New World. From our English roots we have been given the six great gifts of 1) flexibility, 2) emphasis on the Holy Spirit, 3) a love for freedom, 4) movement toward order, 5) the primacy of preaching, and 6) the centrality of the Holy Scriptures.

Now we turn to the second strand that we find in our historical roots. What happened to the new church as she found herself in the New World? What elements in this new unformed land did she appropriate that would shape us to this very day?

If the Old World was ordered and predictable, the New World of the frontier was characterized by unpredictability and great disorder. Worship patterns in the new land were altered drastically by the settlers of the American frontier. We see several qualities that emerged that remain to this day.

Function over aesthetics.—In this new land one of the features which stands out is the emphasis on practicality. Sermons were raw, unfinished documents. The British tradition of written sermons was scrapped. The frontier preacher worked, as did the other members of the community, six hard days a week. He had little time for preparation. He relied heavily on the leadership of the Spirit. The frontiersmen had little time for those things that did not touch their daily lives. Intellect was suspect. Books and learning were not in their frame of reference for the most part. They spent their days on survival. This is what the believers demanded as they hobbled, exhausted, into "the meeting." Small wonder that we have so few examples of 19th-century sermons. Most were not written. The preacher spoke from the heart. Function triumphed over aesthetics.

Meeting houses emphasized practicality.—If their sermons were raw and unfinished, so were their places of worship. They did not have the luxury of relying on symbols. Beauty had little place in the early frontier church. Their buildings were "meeting houses" designed so that people could gather to hear the word of God. Nothing else of consequence was considered by those early settlers.

It is small wonder that we have developed a tradition where people are suspicious of intellect, beauty, and symbolism. Churches have continued to build "auditoriums" where something is heard. Practicality still triumphs in our time. This was one of the legacies of the frontier days.

Shift from God to man.—Perhaps the most profound shift that the frontier brought to the Evangelical Church was its new emphasis on a person-centered worship. One needs only to study the pronouns of the hymn that came from the new land to emphasize this new emphasis. Worship had a new focus: man and his problems and his ills. "I saw the Lord . . ." was shifted to "Brother, are you saved?" Conversion became the central concern of the service. Sermons and services reflected this new emphasis. Most frontier services were revival services that called for the conversion of sinners. The great roots of the faith, held so high in England, were in danger of being extinguished with this shift from God to man. Services were characterized by great outbursts of emotion. These services helped those who lived on the edge of life get through a hard time in a difficult new land.

Out of the richness of our roots in England and the new land, our tradition has come down to us. Any worship must rely on order and freedom if that service is to be whole. Today we find Baptist churches that love order and disdain freedom. We also have many churches that are deeply suspicious of liturgy and yet are freewheeling and freedom loving. Formal and informal structures must flow into our places of worship. Both traditions are essential for a vital worship experience. The old land gave us the great gift of mystery, experimentation, and a love for order. The New World gave us the gift of practicality and evangelism. Those of us that are worship leaders must study carefully these strands that have made us what we are. Only as we incorporate order and freedom will we be able to face the challenges of our age, rooted in the past yet sensitive to the opportunities the Holy Spirit opens up in our time.

Theology and church history help us understand where we came from. Each denomination needs to know its historical and theological roots in order to face the challenges of this age. All of us need to be rooted in the past but open to the new experiences and opportunities the Holy Spirit may bring to us. We now turn to a third foundation stone—the church cannot ignore the local setting of its worship.

Strong Local Traditions

The mistake that many make in worship renewal is that, in their zeal for reform, the leaders forget one of the most important principles: the traditions of the local congregation.

One seminary professor suggested to his class one day that "Just As I Am" would be better placed at the beginning of the service than at the end. He explained that this hymn of consecration would be a good way for worshipers to begin their service. The next Sunday one of his students decided to try this change in his weekend country church. After the call to worship and invocation, he asked his people to turn to "Just As I Am." After the song was sung, the young pastor asked one of the deacons to lead in

prayer. The deacon pronounced the benediction and everyone filed out and went home. The young, green minister had failed to reckon with one of the basic rules of worship: sensitivity to local traditions. That church had
never sung "Just As I Am" anywhere but at the invitation time. They did not understand this change their pastor introduced. Liturgy is not the work of the pastor—but
it is the work of the people.

What are some of the rules that will help the worship
leader in the place where they serve?

Appropriateness for this congregation.—What is suitable in one church may not fit elsewhere. What works
well in some county seat congregation may completely fly
over the heads of those who worship on the edge of town.
It is not that one form of worship is right or wrong as
much as congregations are on different levels. Any worship leader must understand the local traditions.

In the Broadway play, *Fiddler on the Roof*, Tevye and
his people were caught up in a time of change. Russian
Jews were being forced out of their homes to a new place.
The play opens with these words: "And how do we keep
our balance? That I can tell you in a word—tradition!"[11]
Then the villagers take up the theme and sing, over and
over, "Tradition, tradition." The scene finally ends when
Tevye says: "Tradition. Without our traditions, our lives
would be as shaky as—as a fiddler on the roof!"[12] Custom
became the binding tie which kept them going in a very
hard time. In understanding the local traditions of our
people, our worship will provide familiar signposts in a
world where too many things change. Nothing reflects
this more today than an analysis of the customs of your
local congregation.

Plurality of congregation.—Worship leaders would be
surprised by studying the membership rolls in their local
church. The world has changed drastically, and the local
church's membership reflects these changes. Martin

Marty has pointed out this diversity when he studied a statistical sheet of an experimental downtown parish in a metropolitan area. There were 104 members. Eighty-two were considered active. Fifty-four were female; 28 were male; 54 were single, divorced, or widowed; 28 lived over five miles away and, of these, 18 lived over 10 miles away. Twelve of their members were retired; 42 were 45 years of age or older; four were younger than six months; two were over 80; 22 had been members over ten years, and 48 had joined in the last three years. Professions of the members were: seven professors of higher education, six attorneys, six journalists, eight national church body staffers. Marty goes on to say that he believes that any church's membership roll would surprise those who study it.[13]

The needs of any local congregation today are multilayered. There may be a husband and wife and two children sitting down front. But at the end of the 20th century, they will probably be in the minority. You will find your church peopled by singles, divorcees, young people living with grandparents or step-parents. There will be the anxious and the troubled and the desperate sitting there week after week. They come to hear, in their own way, some Word from the Lord.

The worship leader, from start to finish, must consider these multilayered needs. Will the children feel drawn into the circle? Will the singles be left out? Will the old leave the church feeling their church has ignored them? Will the young people be touched?

Our Lord once told a parable about a man who threw out the net and brought back a great variety of fish. And the church today has the very challenging task of flinging out a net large enough to encompass all who come. This is the task of worship in our time.

One of the dangers in considering the local base is that the church is tempted to reflect more of its provincial surroundings than it is that larger kingdom that God has called His people to. So we now turn to some suggestions that we might avoid being too earthbound in our worship.

Escaping the provincial trap.—A seminary professor tells about hitchhiking with a friend in the early 1950s in West Virginia. They were picked up by a serviceman who had just returned from the Korean War. They soon learned this driver was fearless. The center of the highway line meant nothing to him. He carried his assurance in a beer can which he held tightly between his knees. As the tires squealed around the curves, the two young men were afraid they would be hurled into eternity. One of them broke the silence, "Are you a Christian?" Without missing a lick, the driver took a drink from his can and muttered, "Yes, I'm an American."

Paul, in writing to Philippi, reminded those living in that Roman outpost that they were also "God's colony." Philippi prided itself on being a Roman outpost. The people lived as Roman citizens. They adopted Roman customs. They loved their Roman citizenship. There was no doubt that those who lived in Philippi were followers of Rome: their customs, standards, and values. But Paul did not want them to fall into the provincialism trap. Not only were they Roman citizens, but they were members of a larger company—the colony of God. This colony would alter their values and shape their thinking and redirect the allegiances of all their lives.

One of the dangers in considering the local traditions is that one can become so conscious of one's locale that he or she will miss the larger picture. The worship leader's responsibility is to help them realize that they, like Philippi, are part of God's colony.

So worship is different from what happens at the civic club, the school assembly, in television advertising, or the electronic church. Worship is to do for us what it did for Isaiah—it directs us to a seeing we did not have before. It grants us a vision of God, high and lifted up. It touches our lives and the points of our basic needs. We see ourselves as we are. And we are stretched and understand we are part of a very large family—the people of God. How very different from that little company of worshipers who look the same, reflect the same political beliefs, mirror more of their culture than the Christ they serve. Worship must stretch us one and all. In the stretching, we break through the provinciality trap which treats Christ and culture as one and the same.

But there is another principle which the worship leader often overlooks. In fact, there is much in our tradition that would think consideration of beauty in church has little or no place at all.

Strong Artistic Sensitivity

Picture the average church on Sunday. You move your car into the parking lot. What do you see as you drive up? An inviting, well-tended place or is it shabby and poorly kept? As you walk up the steps have the leaves been raked? Has the rice from yesterday's wedding been swept away? Is the shrubbery well-trimmed? As you step into the foyer what is the first thing you notice? Is the building clean and attractive? Do you feel welcome? Someone hands you a bulletin. As you sit in the pew is the program attractive? Are the mistakes obvious? Does this church care about what it does? Is the worship guide easy to read? You look around you. Light shines through the windows. The organ begins to play. There are flowers on the communion table. The choir files in and begins to sing. Does this whole service, its building, and all that makes up this church jar your artistic sensitivity or does it bring you closer to the holy and to the special in life?

Years ago this principle was not quite as important as it is in our time. Even the most remote village has access to a television set. Day after day we are exposed to the slick, well-polished programs and music. Can we expect those raised in a TV age to be anything other than offended if our own efforts do not strive for excellence? Malcolm Muggeridge interviewed Mother Teresa some time ago. He calls the book that came out of that interview, *Something Beautiful for God.* The title comes from her whole philosophy of offering up everything that she does as a gift for God. Mother Teresa is not a physically attractive woman. She is old and wrinkled. Her work is depressing and tedious. She ministers to dying lepers and abandoned children. Where does the beauty come from? Muggeridge says the luminosity of Mother Teresa's life comes from the touch, the care—the dedication and the commitment she gives to all she does. These are the elements that any church, small or large, can follow. We give the best we have to God. Like that widow with her mite, or the boy with his fish, the Lord works a miracle when the sacrifices of His people cost them something. Someone has said, "Worship has to embrace the beautiful, the true, the good. Without a harmonious integration of these elements human worship is going to fall short of its nature and role."[14]

From architecture to cleanliness, from bulletin preparation to flower arranging, we strive to do something beautiful for God. Those worshipers that seek to bring "an offering to the Lord which costs them something" will find themselves, as did Isaiah, caught up, moved, changed by a drama that we find no place else in this world.

Jesus ended His Sermon on the Mount with one great question. Would their foundation be substantive or superficial? Would they construct their faith on rock or sand? Our transitory age cries out for some underpinnings that will last. The challenge before today's church is to provide worship with a strong biblical base, a strong historical base, an understanding of local traditions, and a commitment to artistic sensibility. Such congregations will find they are anchored to a rock. The winds of so much in our time will blow but it will not matter. For their worship will help people in a hard time. They will find the old miracle happening again. They will see their Lord high and lifted up, and it will be enough.

Notes

1. C. S. Lewis, *Letters to Malcom: Chiefly on Prayer* (New York: Harcourt, Brace, 1964), 3.

2. George Adam Smith, *The Book of Isaiah*, vol. 1 (New York: Harper & Brothers, 1927), 56.

3. Susan Rattray, "Worship," *Harper's Bible Dictionary*, Paul J. Achtemeier, ed. (San Francisco: Harper & Row, 1985), 1143.

4. *Ibid.*, 1146.

5. Thomas R. McKibbens, "Our Baptist Heritage in Worship," quoted in *The Review and Expositor*, Southern Baptist Theological Seminary, Louisville, Kentucky, Winter, 1983, 57.

6. Quoted in Carol Doran and Thomas Troeger, *Open to Glory* (Valley Forge: Judson Press, 1983), 70.

7. McKibbens, 58.

8. *Ibid.*, 55.

9. McKibbens, 58.

10. *Ibid.*, 61.

11. Joseph Stein, *Fiddler on the Roof*, (New York: Pocket Books, 1966), 3.

12. *Ibid.*, 10.

13. Quoted in Martin Marty's *Context*, December 1, 1985, 5.

14. Malcom Muggeridge, *Something Beautiful for God* (Garden City, NY: Image Books, 1977), 15.

2

This Is the Word of God

Every renewal of the church in history has been a consequence of men, after a time of deafness, recovering the ears with which to hear not just the words but the strange, disturbing, yet gracious, word that is somehow hidden in the words until it meets the hearer who is ready for it.[1]

—James Smart

And Hilkiah the high priest said to Shaphan the secretary, "I have found the book of the law in the house of the Lord. . . ." Then Shaphan the secretary told the king, "Hilkiah the priest has given me a book." And Shaphan read it before the king. And when the king heard the words of the book of the law, he rent his clothes (2 Kings 22:8,10-11).

Nineteen Seventy-six was an important year for our country. All across America our citizens celebrated the 200th birthday of our freedom. One of the things that our church did was to plan a bicentennial celebration that would reflect Baptist worship 200 years ago. Our worship committee did careful research and one Sunday in July we followed the service of worship our forebears had used in 1776. We discovered that worship began in 1776 when a layperson would bring in the Bible, place it on the pulpit, and open it to the text of the day. Only then was the service ready to begin.

Since our beginnings the Evangelical churches have

slowly moved the Bible further and further from the central place that it once held. There are churches across the land where the Bible is virtually ignored in the worship service. It is strange that the communions which have spent much of their time talking about the importance of the Bible have neglected the very Book they have defended so rigorously. Many churches have very little Scripture read during their services. What is read is often poorly presented to the hearers. The great resources of the Psalms, the Prophets, and much of the Old Testament are virtually ignored. Worship will only be rooted on a solid foundation as we recover, like King Josiah, our central focus on the Holy Scriptures. Just as the structure of the service must reflect the biblical roots of our faith, so the service itself must reflect the Book that binds us together.

Early Hebrew worship clustered around the Torah. This Torah was "instruction" and sometimes called law or revelation. Basically *Torah* meant a narrative, a story rather than a bundle of rules. God's chosen people came together to discover that "God had a story, too." That story took them all in. So the Torah, more than anything else, was a retelling of the beginnings of the people that God called chosen. Israel found her strength for the traumas and catastrophes of life in an old story that began: "In the beginning God. . . . " They survived extinction in 100 different ways because of a Book that kept them going. During and after the awful days of the Exile, the prophets' interpretation of the Torah was their binding tie.[2]

The Psalms became their first book of worship. The Psalter was read daily in the worship of the Temple. Other writings found their place in their public services. The high priest would read aloud from Chronicles, Job, Ezra-Nehemiah, and Daniel. At the various Jewish festivals they would recount the story of the crossing over, the harvest story of Ruth, the sad words of the Lamentations and Ecclesiastes. Esther would be read on some occasions. Through all they did the Psalms flowed like a river.[3]

As we turn to the New Testament we discover that from its very beginning Christianity was also a religion of the Book. One of the extraordinary features of the early church's worship were the numbers of people who were converted by hearing the Old Testament read aloud.[4]

Emerging from its Hebrew roots the early Christian service was patterned after the synagogue service. That service was constructed in this manner:

> First section of the service: Prayer and worship;
> Second section: Reading of the Scripture;
> Third section: Teaching and explanation of the law.

William Barclay has said that it was for the second section that their worship existed. In the reading of the law the whole service reached its center and peak.[5] In the New Testament the congregation was instructed to "attend to the public reading of scripture" (1 Tim. 4:13).[6]

The first description of a Christian worship service appears in the First Apology of Justin Martyr:

> On the day called the Day of the Sun all who live in cities or in the country gather together to one place, and the memoirs of the apostles or the writings of the prophets are read, as long as time permits; then, when the reader has ceased, the president verbally instructs, and exhorts to the imitation of these good things. Then we all rise together and pray.[7]

Robert Webber has pointed out that by the third century the Bible occupied such an important place in worship that often Scripture was read for more than an hour since the people did not possess personal Bibles.

Portions were read from the Law, the Prophets,
the Epistles, Acts, and the Gospels. Between these
readings, lectors would sing psalms or lead the congregation in antiphonal readings or singing of
Scripture.[8]

When Evangelicals began to protest the excesses of the
Roman Church they placed the Scriptures at the heart of
their public worship. Martin Luther ushered in the Reformation with his emphasis on the sole authority of the
Scripture and justification by faith. Zwingli and Calvin
both emphasized the authority of the Scriptures. Calvin
went so far as to say that only those elements clearly defined in Holy Scripture could be part of the service of worship. Zwingli eliminated all music, vestments, the altar,
and most congregational responses from his service.[8]
Early Baptists and other Evangelicals were deeply influenced by Zwingli. An example of how central the Bible
was in those early worship experiences has been noted by
Thomas R. McKibbens:

Solemn prayer by the pastor
  Prophesying (preaching) by pastor for about an
hour on a specific passage of scripture which could
be summarized but not read
  First exhorter preaches on same scripture for
about an hour or as the Spirit leads
  Second exhorter continues to build the sermon for
a similar length of time
  Possibility of other exhortations as the Spirit leads
  Pastor concludes exhortations
  Prayer by the Pastor
  Exhortations for contributions to the poor
  Prayer[10]

From these noble beginnings today's Evangelical
Church must ask what place does the Bible have in our
worship today. James D. Smart has said that this

"strange silence of the Bible in the church" is the greatest
crisis facing the church in our time.

> The church that no longer hears the essential mes-
> sage of the Scriptures soon ceases to understand
> what it is for and is opened to be captured by the
> dominant religious philosophy of the moment, which
> is usually some blend of cultural nationalism with
> Christianity. All distinctions become blurred when
> the voices of the original prophets and apostles are
> stilled.[11]

The worship leader today faces the tremendous challenge of not only bringing the Bible back into the service,
as did our ancestors, but also to place it at the heart of its
worship. The intent of this chapter is to encourage those
interested in the vitality of worship to return the source
of our power to the heart of our worship.

What are some of the ways that the church today can so
elevate the Scriptures that the worshipers can see the
Lord shining through this Word God sends?

Understanding the Nature of Scripture

The first task of the church that would rediscover the
Bible in worship is to consider that the Bible was primari-
ly an oral document. Long before the book was read by
individuals it was read to the congregation. Imagine the
response that the letter to the church at Galatia must
have first evoked when some elder in the church unfolded
that long papyrus scroll and began to read. Place that experience down beside the haphazard, poorly read cluster
of verses that we find in almost any modern worship
hour. We must recover something of the wonder and
freshness that the first hearers found when they opened
the Scriptures. This may not be as difficult as it seems.
Back in the 1970s a theater on Broadway was packed
night after night as a man stood on center stage and

quoted from memory the whole Book of Mark's Gospel. Alex Haley affected a whole nation by telling the story of his *Roots*. If secular audiences can find the power of the Book and meaning in the hearing of another's story told, cannot the local congregation find its way again with a continual meditation on the greatest story ever told?

One of the ways that the Scripture can find meaning today is in an appropriate choice of versions for public reading. With the variety of versions of the Bible in modern English, one must decide carefully which version is suited for public reading. The richness of the *King James Version* cannot be surpassed for beauty. But one might need to turn to the *Revised Standard Version* or other translations for clearer meaning. Sometimes more than one version might be used. Often the meaning of some text will come alive with *The Cotton Patch Version* of certain biblical books by Clarence Jordan or other modern translations. The bottom line in using the Scripture in worship is making sure that the hearers see the Lord high and lifted up, as did Isaiah long ago.

Use a Balance of Scripture

The liturgical church, through the lectionary, suggests a balanced reading of the Old and New Testaments and the Psalms. Whether we use the lectionary approach to the Scriptures or other choices we need to recover a balance in our use of the Scriptures Sunday after Sunday in church.

One of the great strengths of the Evangelical tradition is the infinite variety of ways that a balance of Scripture may be used in our service for power and meaning. One of the psalms might be used as a call to worship. This might be followed later in the same service with an Old Testament reading which could be a confession of sins or even be used as assurance of pardon. The New Testament reading could serve as the reading of the Scripture for the day or even at the time of offering as a Scripture sentence.

Here are some ways that Scriptures might be used to enhance the service.

Calls to Worship

Leader: Lord, thou hast been our dwelling place in all generations.

People: Let thy work appear unto thy servants, and thy glory unto their children.

Leader: And let the beauty of the Lord our God be upon us:

People: And establish thou the work of our hands upon us; yea, the work of our hands establish thou it (Ps. 90:1,16-17,KJV).

Psalm 51 could easily be chosen as a call to worship or as a spoken confession. Here are two examples that could be used on separate Sunday mornings from the same psalm:

Leader: Purge me with hyssop, and I shall be clean;

People: Wash me, and I shall be whiter than snow.

Leader: Fill me with joy and gladness;

People: Let the bones which thou hast broken rejoice.

Leader: Hide thy face from my sins,

People: And blot out all my iniquities.

Leader: Create in me a clean heart, O God,

People: And put a new and right spirit within me.

Leader: Cast me not away from thy presence,

People: And take not thy holy spirit from me.

Leader: Restore to me the joy of thy salvation,

People: And uphold me with a willing spirit (Ps. 51:7-12).

Leader: Create in me a clean heart, O God,

People: And put a new and right spirit within me.

Leader: Then I will teach transgressors thy ways,

People: And sinners will return to thee.

Leader: Deliver me from blood guiltiness, O God, thou
  God of my salvation,
People: And my tongue will sing aloud of thy deliverance.
Leader: Oh Lord, open thou my lips,
People: And my mouth shall show forth thy praise.
Leader: For thou hast not delight in sacrifice;
People: Were I to give a burnt offering, thou wouldst not
  be pleased.
Leader: The sacrifice acceptable to God is a broken spirit,
People: A broken and contrite heart, O God, thou wilt not
  despise (Ps. 51:10, 13-17).

One Sunday morning when I preached on "On Learning How to Die" we began the worship service with these words:
Leader: Let not your hearts be troubled;
People: Believe in God, believe also in me.
Leader: In my Father's house are many rooms;
People: If it were not so, would I have told you that I go to
  prepare a place for you?
Leader: And when I go and prepare a place for you, I will
  come again and take you to myself, that where I am
  you may be also (John 14:1-3).

During a sermon series on the Book of Hebrews these two passages were used on different Sundays to begin our worship:
Leader: Since then we have a great high priest who has
  passed through the heavens, Jesus, the Son of God,
  let us hold fast our confession.
People: For we have not a high priest who is unable to
  sympathize with our weaknesses, but one who in every respect has been tempted as we are, yet without
  sin.
Leader: Let us then with confidence draw near to the
  throne of grace, that we may receive mercy and find
  grace to help in time of need (Heb. 4:14-16).

Leader: Since we are surrounded by so great a cloud of
   witnesses, let us also lay aside every weight, and sin
   which clings so closely,
People: And let us run with perseverance the race that is
   set before us,
Leader: Looking to Jesus the pioneer and perfecter of our
   faith, who for the joy that was set before him endured
   the cross, despising the shame, and is seated at the
   right hand of the throne of God.
People: Consider him who endured from sinners such hostility against himself, so that you may not grow weary or fainthearted (Heb. 12:1-3).

One Sunday when our theme was college ministry, the
service began with an emphasis on the strangers in our
midst:

Leader: Lord, when did we see thee hungry and feed thee,
   or thirsty and give thee drink? And when did we see
   thee a stranger and welcome thee, or naked and
   clothe thee? And when did we see thee sick and in
   prison and visit thee?
People: And the King will answer them, "Truly I say to
   you, as you did it to one of the least of these my brethren, you did it to me" (Matt. 25:37-40).

These are a few of the many ways that the church may
use calls to worship to enhance its worship on a weekly
basis.

Responsive Readings

Many churches do not take full advantage of the responsive readings found in their hymnbooks or their Bibles. Many ignore responsive readings because the congregation responds so poorly. Sometimes the readings
selected are difficult to follow and hard to read. In many
churches the reading in the worship program is printed
in such small type that many in the congregation cannot
decipher the words.

Here are some suggestions as you plan responsive readings.

1. Make sure that the break in the text does not confuse the meaning.
2. Make sure that the Scripture passage lends itself to responsive reading.
3. Offer a variety of ways that the church may hear the Word of God responsively.

Many members of the congregation do not like responsive readings because they are predictable. The leader reads, the people read—Sunday after Sunday. Break up this pattern by using variety in responses. Use two worshipers to read the Scripture passage back and forth. Station one on each side of the pulpit on the floor of the church. Biblical dialogue provides excellent choices for this approach. The story of Adam and Eve talking to God in the Garden might be used. God's encounter with Cain is a possibility. Jesus' dialogue with the scribes and Pharisees could be used and many of the parables. Often the stories come alive when they are broken down between two or more readers. One example of such an approach is found in Isaiah's call in Isaiah 6:1-9:

Reader 1: In the year that King Uzziah died I saw the Lord sitting upon a throne, high and lifted up; and his train filled the temple. Above him stood the seraphim; each had six wings: with two he covered his face, and with two he covered his feet, and with two he flew.

Reader 2: And one called to another and said, "Holy, holy, holy is the Lord of hosts; the whole earth is full of his glory." And the foundations of the thresholds shook at the voice of him who called, and the house was filled with smoke.

Reader 1: And I said: "Woe is me! For I am lost; for I am a

man of unclean lips, and I dwell in the midst of a people of unclean lips; for my eyes have seen the King,
the Lord of hosts!"
Reader 2: Then flew one of the seraphim to me, having in
his hand a burning coal which he had taken with
tongs from the altar. And he touched my mouth and
said: "Behold, this has touched your lips; your guilt is
taken away, and your sin forgiven."
Reader 1: And I heard the voice of the Lord saying,
"Whom shall I send, and who will go for us?' Then I
said, 'Here am I! Send me."
Reader 2: And he said, "Go. . . . "

This approach to responsive readings can be used in a
variety of ways. You might have the choir and minister
read responsively. Sometimes three or four people might
read responsively. You might divide the congregation
right and left and let them read the Scripture for the day.
    With a little creativity and the vast resources of the
Holy Scripture the Bible can come alive through responsive readings.

Using Scripture Sentences

Another way that the Bible can be used in worship is
through Scripture sentences. This can heighten various
aspects of the service. Here are some of the ways you
might use the Bible in meaningful ways in your service.
    Call to Worship.—Begin the service by saying:

O come, let us worship and bow down, let us kneel
before the Lord, our Maker! For he is our God, and
we are the people of his pasture, and the sheep of his
hand (Ps. 95:6-7).

I will lift up my eyes to the hills. From whence does
my help come? My help comes from the Lord, who
made heaven and earth (Ps. 121:1-2).

O come, let us sing to the Lord; let us make a joyful
noise to the rock of our salvation! Let us come into
his presence with thanksgiving; let us make a joyful
noise to him with songs of praise! (Ps. 95:1-2).

They who wait for the Lord shall renew their
strength, they shall mount up with wings like eagles,
they shall run and not be weary, they shall walk and
not faint (Isa. 40:31).

Come to me, all who labor and are heavyladen, and I
will give you rest. Take my yoke upon you, and learn
from me; for I am gentle and lowly in heart, and you
will find rest for your souls. For my yoke is easy, and
my burden is light (Matt. 11:28-30).

Call to prayer.—A beautiful way to begin your prayer
time is in a biblical call to prayer. What better way to
claim the promises of our faith than in some of the great
words of Scripture?

Where two or three are gathered in my name,
there am I in the midst of them (Matt. 18:20).

Ask, and it will be given you; seek, and you will find;
knock, and it will be opened to you (Matt. 7:7).

We have not a high priest who is unable to sympathize with our weaknesses, but one who in every respect has been tempted as we are, yet without sin.
Let us then with confidence draw near to the throne
of grace, that we may receive mercy and find grace to
help in time of need (Heb. 4:15-16).

Assurance of pardon.—People in our churches are
starved for some understanding of forgiveness. At the
heart of our faith there is the wonderful promise that if
we confess, we are forgiven. After a confession time in
your church, sound the good news in a word of pardon.

Come now, let us reason together, says the Lord:
though your sins are like scarlet, they shall be as
white as snow; though they are red like crimson they
shall become like wool (Isa. 1:18).

The Lord is merciful and gracious, slow to anger
and abounding in steadfast love. He will not always
chide, nor will he keep his anger for ever. He does
not deal with us according to our sins, nor requite us
according to our iniquities. For as the heavens are
high above the earth, so great is his steadfast love
toward those who fear him; as far as the east is from
the west, so far does he remove our transgressions
from us (Ps. 103:8-12).

The eternal God is thy refuge, and underneath are
the everlasting arms (Deut. 33:27, KJV).

Stewardship sentences.—What better way to underline
the time for offering than in a Scripture sentence dealing
with our responsibility toward our material possessions.

This is the thing which the Lord has commanded.
Take from among you an offering to the Lord; whoever is of a generous heart, let him bring the Lord's
offering. (Ex. 35:4-5).

Bring the full tithes into the storehouse,. . . and
thereby put me to the test, says the Lord of hosts, if I
will not open the windows of heaven for you and
pour down for you an overflowing blessing (Mal.
3:10).

Do not lay up for yourselves treasures on earth, . . .
but lay up for yourselves treasures in heaven. . . . For
where your treasure is, there will your heart be also
(Matt.6:19-21).

To whom much is given, of him will much be required (Luke 12:48).

Truly, I say to you, as you did it to one of the least of these my brethren, you did it to me (Matt. 25:40).

Lord's Supper.—What more appropriate way do we have to introduce the elements of the Supper than in some relevant Scripture sentence? Sometimes to link the text of the sermon with the verses for the bread and cup underlines the connectedness of every part of the service. Here are some examples that might set you on your own search.

-I-

The Bread.—And he lay down and slept under a broom tree; and behold an angel touched him, and said to him, "Arise and eat." And he looked, and behold, there was at his head a cake baked on hot stones and a jar of water. And he ate and drank, and lay down again (1 Kings 19:5-6).

The Cup.—And the angel of the Lord came again a second time, and touched him, and said, "Arise and eat, else the journey will be too great for you." And he arose, and ate and drank, and went in the strength of that food forty days and forty nights to Horeb the mount of God (1 Kings 19:7-8).

-II-

The Bread.—For he is our peace, who has made us both one, and has broken down the dividing wall of hostility, by abolishing in his flesh the law of commandments and ordinances, that he might create in himself one new man in place of the two, so making peace, and might reconcile us both to God in one body through the cross, thereby bringing the hostility to an end (Eph. 2:14-16).

The Cup.—And he came and preached peace to you who were far off and peace to those who were near; for through him we both have access in one Spirit to the Father. So then you are no longer strangers and sojourners, but you are fellow citizens with the saints and members of the household of God (Eph. 2:17-19).

-III-

The Bread.—Then he poured water into a basin, and began to wash the disciples' feet and to wipe them with the towel with which he was girded (John 13:5).

The Cup.—When he had washed their feet, and taken his garments, and resumed his place, he said to them, "Do you know what I have done to you?" . . . If I then, your Lord and Teacher, have washed your feet, you also ought to wash one another's feet (John 13:12,14).

Benedictions.—We will talk about benedictions in our chapter on prayer. But a few benedictions that might prove meaningful at the end of the service are:

Now unto the King eternal, immortal, invisible, the only wise God, be honor and glory forever and ever. Amen (1 Tim. 1:17, KJV).

The grace of the Lord Jesus Christ, and the love of God, and the communion of the Holy Ghost, be with you all (2 Cor. 13:14, KJV).

The Lord bless you and keep you: The Lord make his

face to shine upon you, and be gracious to you: The Lord lift up his countenance upon you, and give you peace (Num. 6:24-26).

Now unto him that is able to do exceeding abundantly above all that we ask or think, according to the power that worketh in us, Unto him be glory in the church by Christ Jesus, throughout all ages, world without end. Amen (Eph. 3:20-21,KJV).

Music and the Scriptures

Worship leaders have an excellent opportunity to underline the importance of Holy Scripture through the music of the church. The worship leaders would do well to acquaint themselves with the Scripture index at the back of the hymnbook. Much of the great music of the church is rooted in Scripture. Seek creative ways to blend the Scripture for the day with the whole of the service. Churches that aim to lift their congregations beyond the secularity of our time will find help and hope in a return to Scriptures in music. Such an approach will spare the worshipers from mere entertainment and help them blend their voices and yearnings into a praise to Almighty God.

Sermons

The preacher has probably the best opportunity of all to help his people understand and appreciate the Bible through the sermon. Many church members are ignorant of the Bible and its great themes. The sermon, rooted in biblical understanding, can go a long way in creating a love for the Scriptures. When the bread is cast faithfully on the waters it does not return void. P. T. Forsyth has written that "we must all preach to our age, but woe to us if it is our age we preach, and only hold up the mirror to the time."[12] Biblical preaching saves us from being too earthbound and self-centered. The Word of God dissects, separates, convicts, heals, and draws us into the circle of the human family.

One way that the Bible might shape the worship is to begin with the text. Let the text shape the sermon. Then let the sermon text shape all that is done in the worship service. Such a thematic approach gives the worship leader solid resources that will carry the whole of the service.

One Sunday I decided to teach our people something of the wealth of the Psalms. We constructed a whole service around the Psalms that have been meaningful to the people of God. I began with the sermon in my preparation. I entitled the sermon: "Three Kinds of Prayers." We dealt with three types of psalms in the sermon: 1) Psalms of Lamentation; 2) Psalms of Thanksgiving; and 3) Psalms of Worship and Praise. That morning all our choral and instrumental music came from texts of the Psalter. All Scripture passages were from the Psalms. Every hymn was based on a particular Psalm. From start to finish that service focused on the Psalms. In the appendix of this book you will find the order for the Psalm Service. It was our hope that such a service would deepen our congregation's love for this great body of biblical literature.

The same approach of allowing the Scripture to define the sermon and the whole of the service can be used with practically every Scripture passage.

One Lenten season we used the seven last words from the cross as our worship themes. All the services for those seven Sundays clustered around Christ's words from the cross. I called them: "Cross Words." This was the biblical arrangement we used:

> Week 1: "Forgiveness" (Luke 23:26-28)
> Week 2: "Today" (Luke 23:39-43)
> Week 3: "Behold" (John 19:23-27)
> Week 4: "Why?" (Matt. 27:45-50)

Week 5: "Thirst" (John 19:28-30)
Week 6: "Finished" (John 19:25-30)
Week 7: "Father" (Luke 23:46)

The whole of each service was formed around a word from the cross. Such an approach brings the Bible alive for those that gather.

Sermon series are a great way of introducing the Bible to your people. Preach on some book or text for several Sundays. Have all the parts of worship reflect the theme.[13]

Sermons rooted in the authority of the Bible will steer clear of the fads of our time and the whims of the preacher.

There is a great scene in William Faulkner's *The Sound and the Fury*. Dilsey, the elderly maid for the Compton family, wearily trudges down the red-clay road on Easter morning, taking with her the idiot son of the white family she works for. They are on their way to church. That morning, in an ugly little frame church, the preacher arose and began to speak. He spoke of the wonders of Easter and the resurrection and the glory and majesty of Almighty God. After the service ended, old Dilsey takes Benjy and they walk back up the road to her work. She had found something in that service that kept her going. She had met the Word of God face to face and she was able to face the hard things of her life with courage, unafraid.

The worship leader that blends the Word of God to the service will find the old miracle happening again. The Bread of Life, like the old miracle, will be broken and multiplied. All that hear will find all they need for all they must do.

Like our forebearers years ago, bring the Bible back into church. Open the Book and let it work its power. What Isaiah discovered will happen again. People will see the Lord.

Notes

1. James D. Smart, *The Strange Silence of the Bible in the Church* (Philadelphia: The Westminster Press, MCMLXX), 25.
2. James A. Sanders, *Torah and Canon* (Philadelphia: Fortress Press, 1972) 1, 3-9.
3. William Barclay, *The Making of the Bible* (Nashville: Abingdon, 1961), 37-38.
4. Barclay, 41.
5. Barclay, 43.
6. Note also: Acts 13:15; 1 Thessalonians 5:27; Colossians 4:16; Revelation 1:3.
7. Barclay, 44.
8. Robert E. Webber, *Worship Is a Verb* (Waco, Texas: Word Books, 1985), 52.
9. William H. Williamon, *Word, Water, Wine, and Bread* (Valley Forge: Judson Press, 1980), 69.
10. Thomas R. McKibbens, Jr., "Our Baptist Heritage in Worship, *Review and Expositor,* The Southern Baptist Theological Seminary, Louisville, Kentucky, Winter, 1983. 56.
11. James D. Smart, 25.
12. P. T. Forsyth, *Positive Preaching and the Modern Mind* (Grand Rapids, Michigan, Wm. B. Eerdmans Publishing Company, 1966), 5.
13. Sermon series provide a creative way to teach your congregation about the Bible in an intensive way. Here are some of the themes which I have used that I hoped would strengthen our people's understanding of the Word. During these series, worship services were planned around every theme (see appendix).
Hebrews 6: Disciplines of an Undisciplined Age
    Sermon 1: "The Discipline of Transcendence" (Heb. 1:1—2-18)
    Sermon 2: "The Discipline of Obedience" (Heb. 3:1—4:13)
    Sermon 3: "The Discipline of Confidence" (Heb. 4:24—10:18)
    Sermon 4: "The Discipline of Perseverance" (Heb. 10:19—12:29)
    Sermon 5: "The Discipline of the Personal" (Heb. 13:1-21)
A Christmas series focused on the Gospel of Luke as story. Each Sunday I preached on a different story on the Christmas narrative. Each sermon was taken from Luke's Gospel. (See appendix.)
    Advent 1: "Zechariah's Story" (Luke 1:5-25; 57-80)
    Advent 2: "Mary's Story" (Luke 1:26-56; 2:1-7)

Advent 3: "The Shepherd's Story" (Luke 2:8-20)

Advent 4: "Simeon's Story" (Luke 2:22-35)

An exposition of the Book of Galatians connected that great book with the problems the church faces today. The series was entitled: *"A Trumpet for Troubled Times."* (See appendix.)

Sermon 1: "The Problem We All Face" (Gal. 1:1-11)

Sermon 2: "Finding God in Our Stories (Gal. 1:12—2:14)

Sermon 3: "The Heart of the Matter" (Gal. 2:15-21)

Sermon 4: "A Redefinition of the People of God" (Gal. 3:1—4:31)

Sermon 5: "The Art of Hanging in There" (Gal. 5:1—6:10)

3

Let Us Bow Our Heads

Leaving church one Sunday, a member took the pastor's hand and said, "I loved your sermon, but it's the prayers I will remember."

> For we have not a high priest who is unable to sympathize with our weaknesses, but one who in every respect has been tempted as we are, yet without sin. Let us then with confidence draw near to the throne of grace, that we may receive mercy and find grace to help in time of need (Heb. 4:15-16).

The year was 1978. It was a Sunday summer afternoon. We were scheduled to baptize that evening. But there was a hitch. Someone had forgotten to fill the baptistry. There was no water. We had planned the service carefully around one particular young man who would be baptized. His father was seriously ill with cancer. We had structured this service between chemotherapy treatments when the father was not so sick. We had asked that man to have the baptismal prayer for his son and the other candidates. So, as happens often in the church, we had to come up with a contingency plan. We called a family with a swimming pool and asked them if we could have our service there. I was heartsick. My own son was to be baptized. This man with cancer had come with great pain to see his own son baptized. I could just see people standing around snickering. But such was not the case. Something happened that sunny afternoon. The grace of God moved

54

among us. None of us present will ever forget that particular baptism. One of the things that made the service so
special was the bald-headed father dying of cancer. He
pulled from his pocket a prayer he had written for his
nine-year-old son and the other candidates. This is what
he prayed:

> Heavenly Father, at this time we would like to
> dedicate these young people to You as they choose to
> become members of Your intimate family through
> the sacrament of baptism. Remember how You led
> Your chosen people out of Egypt by Your show of
> power at the waters of the Red Sea? Please show the
> same power for these boys tonight and protect them
> as You protect all of Your children. Remember how
> You led Your chosen people through the waters of
> the river Jordan to let them enter the promised
> land? Please lead these boys through the trials and
> joys of life to the heaven You promise to those who
> follow Your way. Remember how You gave salvation
> to the world by the blood and water that flowed from
> Your Son's side on the cross? Please give the same
> salvation to these boys as they enter the waters of
> baptism as Your adopted sons. Remember how You
> sent the Holy Spirit to Your close followers on Pente-
> cost and gave them the courage to be brave Chris-
> tians in their words and actions. Please send the
> same Holy Spirit into these boys tonight so that they
> can carry out Your teachings in their lives. Be with
> us all, Heavenly Father, so that we can also live out
> the power of our baptism in our own lives. Amen.[1]

No one present will ever forget that special moment.
After the service this man took all the children who had
been baptized out for a celebration at a fast-food restau-
rant. It was this man's last public appearance. He died a
few months later.

One of the earliest accounts we have of early Christian

worship is found in Acts 2 where Luke wrote: "And they devoted themselves to the apostles' teachings and fellowship, to the breaking of bread *and the prayers*" (v.42, author's italics). There is no real worship without that special time when the people of God lift up their praise and petitions to Almighty God.

The Scriptures are filled with a variety of prayers—adoration, confession, pardon, thanksgiving, submission, dedications, petition, supplication, and meditation.

During the Reformation the Reformers reacted strongly against the musty traditions of the prescribed prayer. In revolt against the excesses of formalism, some Reformers opted for extemporaneous prayers. But history shows that John Calvin, in his Reformed congregation in 1542, adopted what has been called "the Genevan order."

> Scripture sentence: Psalms 124:8
> Confession of sins; Prayer for pardon
> Metrical Psalm sung by the congregation
> Prayer for illumination
> Scripture Reading
> Sermon
> Collection
> Intercessions
> Lord's Prayer, in long paraphrase
> Apostles' Creed
> Communion (when observed)
> Words of Institution
> Exhortation
> Consecration prayer
> Communion (psalm sung or scriptures read)
> Post-communion prayer
> Benediction[2]

We find that there were seven prayers in that service and each prayer was a different kind of prayer.

In 1768 Morgan Edwards, former pastor of the First

Baptist Church in Philadelphia, designed the following
service which was used by many Free Church congregations. Richard Furman, longtime pastor of the First Baptist Church, Charleston, South Carolina was deeply influenced by Morgan Edwards's service. This was how that
service was structured.

> A short prayer, suitably prefaced
> Reading of Scripture
> A longer prayer
> Singing (congregational)
> Preaching
> A third prayer
> Singing
> The Lord's Supper (on appointed Sundays)
> Collecting for the necessities of saints
> Benediction[3]

We find at least four separate and distinct prayers in
this service of worship.

In both of these services we see that prayer was a vital
part of worship. Each prayer had a different purpose. If
prayer is to be a real part of our worship today we must
come to some understanding of the types of prayers that
have been part of the believers' worship through the
years.

Preparation

One of the dangers of the Evangelical Church is that
prayers are handled so casually. We would not think of
meeting with the President of the United States without
a purpose for the meeting. Yet we often come into the
holy of holies casually and ill-prepared.

The issue is not if we are to write or not write our
prayers. The larger issue is preparation. Long before the
service begins the worship leader should have a clear idea
of what he or she will pray in different parts of the

service.

Types of Prayers

Even the most loosely structured services incorporate a rich variety of prayers. What better way to teach the congregation about prayer than by modeling prayer by a variety of prayers used during the worship service? Here are some of the prayers that can breathe vitality into any service.

Invocations.—The invocation *invokes* the Spirit of God as the service begins. This is not the time to pray for missionaries, a general thanksgiving, but the moment when we ask God to bless our efforts and meet us where we are.

Here are some examples that I have used during this time of the service:

Lord—
We come to worship You . . .
We come to praise Your name . . .
We come to find Your will . . .
We come to know Your great peace.
So take these moments before us and blend us into a family of seekers.
Then, meet us here . . . speak to whatever it is we bring and help us to know that we are not alone in what we do. Amen.

Loving Father—
Meet here in this place. Take away our sin. Show us how great is the distance between what we dream and what we do. Whisper peace to our worries and fears until we grow quiet within. And then send us on our way—more than conquerors—not on our own—but through the strong name of Jesus our Lord. Amen.

Loving Father—

Make us conscious right now of what great treasures we
hold in our hands. This day will not come back again.
When it is gone—it is gone. As we continue to open the
package of this day—help us to handle with care the life
that we have been given. Some things are cumbersome
and hard; some are wondrous and special. Let none slip
through our fingers without a benediction and a recogni-
tion of the goodness of life itself. We thank You for it all.
Amen.

Lord God—
          Take us as we are and do with us what needs to
be done.
Some of us need encouragement . . .
     Some of us need forgiving . . .
          Some of us need to hear news that is good . . .
               Some of us need to know that we are loved . . .
          Some of us find it hard to identify where we
are and what we need.
But we come just as we are. Receive us, change us, help
us, and meet us here. Amen.

Here is one invocation that I prayed during the Advent
season:

Lord God—
          Help us to open wide the deep places of our
hearts this morning. That Christmas will flow down into
our every crevice of our beings.
          That we may be delivered from whatever it is
that makes us less than human and less that You intended us to be.
          And if some of us bring fear, may we hear an an-
gel say: "Fear not . . ."
          If some of us bring sins, may we hear: "Your sins
are forgiven . . ."

If some of us bring a grief, may we hear: "Surely he has borne our griefs . . ."

We thank You for the great promise of hope and salvation that Your Son brings. Amen.

One springtime I began the service with this invocation:

> Around us, Lord—the world is stirring again. The trees bud, the flowers begin to bloom. The grass turns green. Beauty is breaking forth among us. We need a stirring within. Move among the things that are dead . . . the parts of us that seem so hopeless. Make springtime come inside. Renew us. Make us new creatures in Christ Jesus. This is why we are here. Amen.

The Lord's Prayer.—Counseling a young couple about to be married, I asked them what were the most meaningful parts of worship for them. The young man said the most moving part of the service for him was the Lord's Prayer. Every Sunday, following the invocation, the congregation prays the Lord's Prayer together. What better way to lift up the longings of the people than through the model that Jesus gave us?

Some churches have found Mallotte's musical version of the Lord's Prayer a beautiful way to pray the prayer. Prepare your congregation ahead of time, then let the organist sound a chord following the invocation and let the people sing the prayer in unison. I have discovered that when the Lord's Prayer becomes part of our weekly worship, members ask for this prayer on other occasions.

One way to incorporate this prayer is at weddings and funerals. The whole of life can be gathered up in this Model Prayer Christ left for the church.

Prayers of confession.—The Evangelical Church has long been suspicious of confession. Remembering the excesses of the church in former days, many believers

feared the very word *confession* in church. Yet believers
need some time to confess their sins of omission and com-
mission. Sometimes confession may be silent, other times
the prayer may be typed and included in the printed order of worship.

One confession that could be used is:

> Lord, have mercy upon us.
> Christ, have mercy upon us.
> Forgive us our trespasses, our Father,
> against Thee: _____
> against ourselves: _____
> against life: _____
> against others: _____
> as we forgive those who trespass against us.

One Sunday when I preached on "Making The Connections," our congregation prayed this confession together:

> Leader: Forgive us, O Lord our transgressions:
> People: This failure of ours to make connections.
> Leader: For saying the words
> People: And ignoring the deeds;
> Leader: For meeting to worship
> People: And ignoring real meeting outside this
> place;
> Leader: For singing hymns on Sunday
> People: And blurring the words on Monday;
> Leader: For talking love
> People: And failing to love;
> Leader: For using what we have on ourselves
> People: And forgetting a world in need;
> Leader: For hearing your word
> People: And ignoring its work in our lives;
> Leader: For failing to see the ties between Sunday
> and weekday
> People: Good Lord, hear our prayers and forgive us
> all our sins.

One meaningful way to deal with confession in the worship service is to let the congregation sing the confession. Ken Medema's chorus, "Lord, Make Me Clean," could be easily taught and sung by the congregation in the service.[4]

Another way for the church to pray a prayer of confession is to use David's great confessional prayer in Psalm 51. The Psalm can be used and prayed together or divided between leader and people.

One of the most memorable confession times we have had in our church occurred on a Maundy Thursday evening. That evening I preached on "Surely he has borne our griefs and carried our sorrows. . . ." After the sermon, before Communion, we gave each worshiper a piece of paper, a pencil, and a straight pin attached to the paper. Then we took a few minutes and wrote out our individual confessions. After they were written, the people came forward and pinned them to the cross at the front of the sanctuary. After they had made their confessions, they moved to the table and received the Lord's Supper.

Pardon.—Each confession should end with a pardon from the Scriptures. What better way to lift up the burdens of the people than with the pardoning word of good news. Here are some examples:

> The sacrifice acceptable to God is a broken spirit; a broken and contrite heart, O God, thou wilt not despise (Ps. 51:17).

> If we confess our sins, he is faithful and just, and will forgive our sins and cleanse us from all unrighteousness (1 John 1:9).

> He does not deal with us according to our sins, nor requite us according to our iniquities. For as the heavens are high above the earth, so great is his steadfast love toward those who fear him; as far as

the east is from the west, so far does he remove our transgressions from us (Ps. 103:10-12).[5]

Silent prayers.—People in our culture are starved for silence. Indeed, silence is so rare that to interject it into a service of worship without preparation makes many worshipers extremely nervous. One pastor took a survey of the parts of his service of worship that were most meaningful to his people. He was amazed to discover that the time of silent prayer was the most important part of his church's corporate worship experiences.

Churches that incorporate periods of silence in their services offer the worshipers opportunities to confront mystery in a special way. What other place in our harried society offers such opportunity?

One way to incorporate silence in the service is with the guided prayer. Here the worship leader will direct the prayer for the day, yet the people do their own praying. Here is one example of the guided prayer.

> Let us thank God for the blessings of our lives.
> (Pause)
> Let us thank God for some special event or friend who has graced us in the last week.
> (Pause)
> Let us thank God for Jesus Christ and for the love that He holds out to us today.
> (Pause)
> Let us pray for a world in need.
> (Pause)
> Let us remember those in this community who work hard for peace and justice.
> (Pause)
> Let us remember those caught up in systems they cannot change.
> (Pause)

Let us pray for all those who do not know the Lord
Jesus Christ.
(Pause)
Let us pray for our own needs here.
(Pause)
Let us ask God to forgive us of our sins.
(Pause)
Let us pray for the person on our right and left—
the one in front and back.
(Pause)
May Christ's life touch us all here and now and
meet all our needs. Amen.

But the most meaningful of the silent prayers may be
just to ask your members to bow their heads and bring the
concerns of their lives and world to the care and keeping
of the Father. The problem with so many churches that
employ silence is that they do not give their people
enough time to pray. Make these moments long enough
that the people will have time to bring their needs to the
throne of grace. Some churches punctuate their silence
with organ music or a quiet choral selection. I personally
find this approach to silence distracting. Let the worshiper be confronted with some time in the service when he or
she must stand without anything between them and the
Holy. Such moments, in time, may prove to be one of the
high moments in the worship service.

Pastoral prayers.—One of the most powerful parts of
some worship services is when the pastor leads his people
in the pastoral prayer. What was said of Dr. Fosdick may
be said of us, "I loved your sermon, but it is the prayers
that I will remember." Perhaps no part of worship is
more neglected in the Evangelical Church than the pastoral prayer. Historically, this has been the time when the
pastor will lay the needs of his people and the world before God. Such a prayer should be carefully planned and
be one of the most intimate parts of worship.

Dr. Ernest Campbell, has given us an excellent model for pastoral prayers in his little book called, *Where Cross the Crowded Ways of Life.* He structures his pastoral prayer into three sections: Thanksgiving, Intercession and Petition.[6] The worship leader could learn much about pastoral prayers by studying Dr. Campbell's prayers in this book. Here is an example of one pastoral prayer he prayed while minister of the Riverside Church:

I

O Thou who art the hope of all who seek Thee, and the joy of all who find; even on our darkest days we have cause to praise Thy name:

that there should be a universe at all;

that we should be granted the incredible miracle of life;

that we should be able to perceive purpose and design, notice beauty, feel and communicate joy;

that we should know ourselves free and responsible;

that we should be upheld by a love we often spurn, and overturned again and again by a Spirit we frequently resist;

that there is healing for our hurts, comforts for our sorrows, light for our darkness, and pardon for our sins.

O Lord, our Lord, how excellent is Thy name in all the earth. Take to Thy self the thanks we raise to Thee.

Through Jesus Christ our Lord.

II

Here is this house of prayer we would pray for all who are fast becoming slaves of unworthy masters:

those who are leaning more and more on the glass crutch of alcohol;

those whose style of life is increasingly controlled by peer-group pressures;

those whose daily work kills the soul inch by inch;

those for whom money has passed from a means to an end;

those who have become so dependent on order that they can only curse the new, and fear it;

those who are formally committed to loyalties they no longer feel;

those in public office who find their political debts stifling their ability to say and do what's right.

O thou who are more willing to set us free than we are to walk in freedom, show us Thy love and in Thy mercy save us.

Through Jesus Christ our Lord. Amen.[7]

III

Lord, in the quiet of this hour before Thee, we would pause to ask for a surer knowledge of who we are and what we are about.

If we can recall a time when we loved Thee more, restore.

If we have become good friends with some favorite sin, rebuke.

If the flame of commitment to the world's awful need flickers dimly, rekindle.

If along the way a relationship once cherished stands endangered through some wrong, real or imagined, reunite.

Show us the relevance of Christ for the life we live within and the world we make for others, that we may no longer live to ourselves but unto Him whom we call Savior, Lord, and Friend.

Through Jesus Christ our Lord. Amen.

Dr. Stephen F. Olford has written about attending Westminster Chapel where Martyn Lloyd-Jones was the

minister. He reports that to hear Dr. Jones pray, sometimes from 20 to 25 minutes, was to be lifted in the Spirit
to the throne room of heaven. He said that after such a
prayer that a sermon was hardly necessary. Dr. Olford
writes that the pulpit prayers of Charles Haddon Spur-
geon were of the same order.[8] Ernest Campbell has said
that any minister who wishes to invigorate his congregation should think of energizing the usual instead of sched-
uling the unusual.[9] Perhaps the vitality will return to our
corporate worship as we begin to recover the importance
of the pastoral prayer in the life of the church.

Intercessory prayers.—Sometimes intercession can be
incorporated into the pastoral prayer and sometimes this
prayer may be a separate part of the service. But intercessory prayer is that time when the people of God intercede
before the Almighty for some person or need.

Lyle Schaller, church consultant, has said that the past
two decades have brought a renewed interest in intercessory prayer in most churches. He says that the dominant
Christian trend for the last third of this century may be a
rediscovery of the Holy Spirit. But he says that scientifi-
cally trained adults are discovering that we really are dependent on God and not simply ourselves. He states that
people in our time seem to be starved for transcendence.
Thus, churches are rediscovering the validity of intercessory prayer.[10]

Dr. Schaller says that in many services that the minister will leave the pulpit and move into the congregation,
asking for prayer requests among the membership. Then
he incorporates these petitions into the pastoral prayer.

Schaller says that some churches place a large cork
bulletin board in the foyer and invite those worshiping to
write their prayer requests down as they enter the
church. Ushers collect these during the first hymn and
bring them to the minister who incorporates them into
his pastoral prayer. Another way of doing this is to place

prayer request cards in the pew racks. Worshipers are invited to fill out these cards before the service begins. Ushers collect them and the pastor weaves these petitions into the pastoral prayer.[11]

Whatever method you use in your church, there should be some way that the needs of the people are lifted up to the care of the Father. In my own congregation we place the names of those in the hospital and with special needs in the bulletin under the prayer time. We also recognize those married that week and those who have lost loved ones. Sometimes those that have just celebrated a 50th wedding anniversary or retired are remembered. Often I call their names and lift up their joys and needs during the pastoral prayer. The church that remembers its people in prayer during the junctures of their lives will never go out of business.

Offertory prayers.—Many churches ask laypersons to pray this prayer every Sunday. This is a time when we thank God for the gifts of our lives. It is also an opportunity when we ask Him to take the loaves and fish that we bring and multiply and scatter them once again.

Some of the most moving moments we have had in our worship have been when some layperson has come forward, taken the microphone, and led us in the offertory prayer. Some of those prayers have brought tears to my eyes. Liturgy becomes the work of the people.

Another way to pray during this time is to let the whole congregation pray as one. There are many prayers that may be offered by the body and written out in your order of service. Lee Phillips's work may be helpful here as you work out your own prayers.

Merciful God,
Teach us to give first from love,
Not from any other motive:
Our love for Thee,
Our love for others,

The proper love for ourselves.
Then show us as we give from love
There is always more to give!
Amen.[12]

Teach us, Holy God,
That true giving is not measured
By what is given,
But by what is left;
Not quantity but quality;
Not size but sacrifice.
Through Him who counted not the cost
Yet freely gave His life
A ransom for sinners.
Amen.[13]

Special Prayers.—We must not overlook the special days in the life of the church. Such occasions as note burnings, dedication of a new building, parent and child dedication services, baptismal services, and other events offer the church great opportunities to bring to the altar the changing events of our lives. Some of these events are made more special when a layperson in the congregation leads the prayer. Once I asked a speech professor who was a member of our congregation to lead us in prayer when we dedicated a new pulpit in the church. This was the prayer she prayed that morning:

Father, many of us are thinking that the dedication of a pulpit is a bit unusual but really rather nice; help it to be also meaningful. Enable us—right now to make of these moments a time of confession and commitment. Help us to accept this pulpit as a symbol of your continuing revelation of yourself through the Bible, yes, but also through your Holy Spirit dwelling in and moving through our pastor and through each of us as we grow in love for you and for each other. May the voice from this pulpit be one of challenge as well as comfort; a voice which reveals a personal questing after truth as well as one which admonishes us with wise counsel. We pray that this will not be a place where the easy word is heard—nor the empty phrase. . . . We need to be led in the way of openness. We're scared that if the person beside us right now knew us as we know ourselves he would despise us. So we hide ourselves from the very persons we call brothers and sisters in Christ.

From time to time, Father, there are those who enter our doors who are searching desperately for someone to love them—for some place to belong. May the voice from this pulpit offer these lonely ones the assurance that Christ can heal deep and angry wounds, that He can bind up the broken—and give rest to the weary—that He already loves them. May the voice speak for us our offer of friendship—our willingness to be one with them in a fellowship of faith.

There are others who come and sit among us who doubt the resurrection power because they have failed to see evidence of that power in our lives who say we believe. May the voice from this pulpit invite them to remain among us, to challenge us and help us face our hypocrisies. And may they begin to realize that it is we who have failed—not Christ. Teach us to be honest with you and with them.

May the voice from this pulpit lead us to an awareness of the wonderful freedom we have in Christ—a freedom to love each other, to be ourselves, creatively and intellectually to search out truth—to know experientially—for ourselves—the power and peace of the Holy Spirit, the freedom to go beyond these doors, to move in Christ's name among persons who have such tearing and hurting needs, the freedom to care—to run the risk of misunderstanding in order to do what we believe you want us to do.

Help us, Father, to acknowledge our responsibility

to the ones who stand in this pulpit. Help us to com-
mit ourselves to prayer and to participation in worship. Help us to have hearing ears and seeing eyes
and searching minds and loving hearts. Help us to
share in the strains and struggles of this place as
well as in the joys and victories. Teach us to pray and
to care about what happens here. Help us to come to
worship with a sense of expectancy and gladness.
Teach us to be still when we should be still and to act
when we should act. Teach us to pray and to love. To
these purposes we dedicate this pulpit and ourselves
in Jesus' name. Amen.[14]

Benedictions.—As the service is about to end, the benediction is sounded. This is when we ask God to bless His
people as they move outside the church building and into
the world. Sometimes the benediction may be a summing
up of what has been done and said. But it should not be
long and should bring to closure the whole of the service.

I end every service with the same benediction: "And
now may the peace which passes all understanding and
the love that will not let us go, abide with us both now and
forevermore. Amen." This benediction has become a favorite of many of our members. Our teenagers love it especially. It has been used as the text for several funerals
for senior adults because they requested it before they
died. James Bennett, minister of music at the First Baptist Church of Clemson, South Carolina has set this benediction to music.[15]

A Blessing

Roger Lovette   James Bennett

May the peace that pass - es un - der - stand - ing,___ And the

love that will nev - er let you go; May they

rest and a - bide with you now and for -

ev - er - more! A - men.

Many biblical benedictions are found throughout the Scriptures.[16] A favorite benediction for many people was popularized by Dr. John Claypool when he was pastor of Crescent Hill Baptist Church in Louisville, Kentucky. He concluded the service with this benediction:

> Depart now in the fellowship of God the Father, and as you go remember, in the goodness of God you were brought into this world. By the grace of God you have been kept even to this very moment; and, by the love of God, fully revealed in the face of Jesus Christ, you are being redeemed. Amen.

The church that takes its corporate prayer life seriously provides its people with a powerful ally for the days ahead. The people know that they do not go alone. They have lifted up their voices in prayer together to Almighty God. He has heard their petitions. They are prepared for whatever life brings.

Notes

1. Prayer written by Dr. Bernie Caffrey.
2. Donald P. Hustad, "Baptist Worship Forms: Uniting the Charleston and Sandy Creek Traditions," *Review and Expositor* (Winter, 1988), 38.
3. Hustad, 32.
4. Ken Medema, *The Gathering* (Waco, Texas: Word Incorporated, 1977), 24f.
5. Other Scriptures that may be used at the time of pardon are: Jeremiah 31:33-34; Psalm 103:8; Psalm 103:3-5; Isaiah 57:18; 1 Chronicles 7:14; Isaiah 43:25; John 3:16; Isaiah 43:2; Isaiah 44:21-22; Isaiah 53:4-6.
6. Ernest Campbell, *Where Cross the Crowded Ways* (New York: Association Press, 1973), 7.
7. *Ibid.*, 46-47.
8. Stephen F. Olford, "Restoring the Scriptures to the Baptist Worship," *Review and Expositor,* Winter, 1988, 24.
9. Campbell, 7-8.

10. Lyle E. Schaller, *44 Ways to Increase Church Attendance,* (Nashville: Abingdon Press, 1988), 33-34.

11. *Ibid.,* 34-35.

12. E. Lee Phillips, *Breaking Silence Before the Lord* (Grand Rapids, Michigan, 1986), 107.

13. *Ibid.,* 111.

14. Prayer by Edwina Hunter.

15. Music by James Bennett. Permission to use this benediction may be obtained by writing: Mr. James Bennett, First Baptist Church, 396 College Avenue, Clemson, SC 29631.

16. Other biblical benedictions that you might use are: Matthew 28:19-20; Romans 16:25-27; 1 Corinthians 16:13-14; 2 Corinthians 13:11; Galatians 6:9-10; Philippians 3:8; 1 Thessalonians 5:23; 2 Thessalonians 3:16; Philemon 1:25; Hebrews 13:20-21; 1 Peter 2:9-10; 2 Peter 3:18.

4

A Faith that Sings

The lights went out, and the children's choir began its slow march up the aisle, holding candles and singing . . . "To our home on the prairie, sweet Jesus has come. Born in a stable, he blesses his own. Though humble our houses and fortunes may be, I love my dear Savior who smiles on me"—and in the dark, the thin sweet voices and illuminated faces passing by, people began to weep. The song, the smell of pine boughs, the darkness, released the tears they evidently had held back a very long time. Her mother wept, her father who had given me stony looks for hours bent down and put his face in his hands.

—Garrison Keillor[1]

And it was the duty of the trumpeters and singers to make themselves heard in unison in praise and thanksgiving to the Lord), and when the song was raised, with trumpets and cymbals and other musical instruments, in praise to the Lord, "For he is good,/ for his steadfast love endures for ever,"/ . . . the house of the Lord, was filled with a cloud, so that the priests could not stand to minister because of the cloud; for the glory of the Lord filled the house of God (2 Chron. 5:13-14).

Picture the scene. It is Saturday afternoon. The church is decorated in greenery and flowers and candles. In just a few minutes the music will start, the bridesmaids and ushers will file in, and the bride will come down the long center aisle on her father's arm. Those gathered will open hymnals and sing: "All creatures of our God and King, Lift up your voice and with us sing Alleluia! Alleluia!" As the service ends, someone will sing, "The Lord's Prayer." The groom kisses the bride and the organ recessional sounds. From beginning to end, music flows like a river through that wedding service.

The scene shifts to Monday afternoon. In the same church another company gathers. This time the mood is somber. A faithful member of the church for over 50 years has died. Friends come to pay a final tribute. At this time the worshipers open their hymnals and sing, "The Lord is my shepherd. . . ." Music helps the people express what they find so hard to put into words.

The next Sunday we return to that same sanctuary. The service begins with baptism. A nine-year-old girl is being baptized and a 24-year-old father. After the minister has said: "Upon the profession of your faith in the Lord Jesus and in obedience to His commands . . ." he baptizes these two converts. As they leave the water, the congregation sings again. "Happy day, happy day, When Jesus washed my sins away!" Music heightens these conversion experiences by helping all present to express praise and thanksgiving.

We cannot imagine the faith journey without music. From early biblical history music has served many purposes: merrymaking at social occasions, noisemaking in times of war, magical incantation, and the worship of God.

Little is known of music in early Hebrew worship. Only as we come to the time of David do we find music occupying a strategic place in the religious life of the people. But even there music was relegated to a secondary role. Sacrifice was the primary thrust of worship.

Through the years their music changed. Culture affected the synagogue service. As would happen in every age,

slowly their music bore the distinct stamp of their particular day and age.

New Testament church music can be linked to music
we find in the synagogue. Various epistles allude to the
music of the church—but we are unclear as to the place of
music in the New Testament era. We do know: 1) They
emphasized organized prayer and songs as opposed to
spontaneous worship patterns; 2) There was a tension between biblical songs and extrabiblical literature; 3) As
Gentiles gained power in the church they brought with
them a Hellenistic influence which can be seen in their
music; 4) Early Christians struggled to decide if vocal music was more important than instrumental music.[2]

But all this is background. Early Baptists, we have already seen, scorned any order. Music was important to
John Smyth and his congregation. But words and tunes
were likely memorized. Members of the congregation
probably sang extemporaneously as they chose.

By the latter part of the 17th century, controversy began to swirl around music in the church. Pastor Benjamin Keach began to write hymns and in 1693 22 members
of his church at Horsley Down left and sought membership in the Bagnio Church. These believers were not used
to any hymns that were not taken directly from the
psalms of the Bible. They saw any other lyrics as "a hu-
mane invention."[3]

But Pastor Keach continued to write lyrics to be sung
in public worship. He was the first to introduce hymns
into the regular worship of an English congregation of
any kind. His 1691 hymnbook, *Spiritual Melody*, was the
first hymnbook to be used in Great Britain.[4]

When Baptists moved from the Old World to the frontier, they found the new land drastically altering their
worship patterns. Music, too, became a reflection of the
New World. The greatest shift can probably be seen in

their hymnbooks. Before 1807 most of their songs emphasized God and praise.[4] After that the focus was on man-
kind, their feelings, needs, and responses. Singing became lively and emotional and the young church in
America began to focus on conversion far more than
praise.

So the strands of order and freedom, formality and in-
formality, ancient hymns, and new gospel songs have
come down to us. Today's Evangelical Church reflects all
these strands in its worship and music.

But something else has occurred. Many feel that today
is a difficult time for church music. Ours could well be
called the decade of experiment. Probably nothing has altered the average person's perception today as much as
new musical forms and television. In the late 1960s and
70s something new emerged in church music. The sound
of the world affected the church in perhaps a more dra-
matic way than ever before. We began to hear of "contemporary gospel music." One could close one's eyes and hear
country-and-western melodies in many sanctuaries. Gospel rock, romantic songs sung to the Almighty, folk tunes,
praise choruses, and refrains repeating the same verse of
Scripture over and over could be heard. Hymnbooks have
been replaced with overhead projectors for many congregations. Amplifiers, sound systems, and mixers came to
be as important as organs. Some churches have bragged
that they have not sung a hymn in months. Orchestras,
tambourines, and taped music can be heard in churches
throughout the land. What are we to say to all of this
change? Is it good or bad?

A Blending of Old and New

From earliest times there has been a tension in music.
The struggle has been to hold on to the old or to embrace
the new. Culture has had a way of changing and altering

all of life—even worship. We see this in early Hebrew history when Solomon's wife brought with her from her foreign land 1,000 musicians. We see culture changing the
church when the Gentiles introduced Hellenistic ideas
into worship and music. Martin Luther turned the
church inside out by asking: "Why should the devil have
all the best tunes?" And Isaac Watts would swim against
the tide and finally win with his hymns to Almighty God.
Blind Fanny Crosby would revolutionize evangelical worship with her hymns from the heart. One wonders as the
church today struggles with the new sounds of contemporary music how much of the old struggles of yesterday
can be seen in our own time. Will our tensions with music
be creative or destructive? Will the church of the 21st
century be better served because of the changes that music has evoked in our time? We do not know the answers
but we can ask some basic questions about what we do
and where we are. We must be careful not to discard the
old or to ignore the new.

The old.—Our disposable society cries out for something that lasts. The old hymns and anthems of yesterday
can give the church some stability it hungers for. Dan
Wakefield has touched our pulse today when he writes:

> Many of us become wanderers, moving from city to
> city and job to job (as well as marriage to marriage,
> even family to family) as part of an accepted nomad-
> ic lifestyle instead of putting down roots in one place,
> with one permanent wife or husband and set of chil-
> dren, working for one company—or, as it was more
> appropriately called in the old days, a "firm." It is
> little wonder that many of us become psychically dis-
> oriented, in need of medical or psychological "treat-
> ment," and suffer from a spiritual vacuum where
> our center should be.[5]

Martin Rinkart's, "Now Thank We All Our God" written in that terrible 16th century of the black plague, can teach us how to give a proper thanks in a hard time. Martin Luther's, "A Mighty Fortress Is Our God" can help us recover our perspective again. Harry Emerson Fosdick's, "God of Grace and God of Glory" can give us vision for the days ahead. The simple "Doxology" can help us recover a sense of gratitude for the simplest things. Choirs and congregations must keep much of the past lest faith become rootless and only instant gratification.

The new.—The challenge of contemporary music is to speak to the needs of the people. It is to meet people on their level. It is to express the gospel in ways that can be understood.

Robert Dale has said that congregational singing can be a powerful tool in helping us shape our theology and kingdom dreams.[6] Recently our congregation learned a new English chorus which became the theme for our stewardship emphasis and beginning of a new ministry for pastor and people. One week the choir sang the chorus for a call to worship. Then the people learned the song, and sang it as a call to worship, another Sunday at the offering time, one Sunday as a congregational hymn, and another Sunday as the invitational hymn. It will be a long time before our congregation forgets the dream of those simple words:

> We shall be as one,
> We shall be as one,
> He the Father of us all.
> We His chosen sons;
> And by His command
> Take each other's hand.
> Live our lives in unity,
> We shall be as one.
>
> We shall be as one,

We shall be as one,
And by this shall
all men know
Of the work He has done.
Love will take us on
Through His precious
Son;

Love of Him who first loved us
We shall be as one.[7]

Another new hymn which many congregations are just
discovering was written by Ken Medema and is sung to
Martin Luther's, "A Mighty Fortress Is Our God." This
strong hymn can be used with great effect.

In unity we lift our song of grateful adoration,
For brothers brave and sisters strong
What cause for celebration.
For those whose faithfulness has kept us through
distress,
Who've shared with us our plight, Who've held us
in the night,
The blessed congregation.

For stories told and told again to every generation,
To give us strength in times of pain,
To give us consolation.
Our spirits to revive to keep our dream alive,
When we are far from home and evil seasons come;
How firm is our foundation.

For sacred scriptures handed down, a blessed trust
and treasure,
Which gives us hope when hope is gone
And makes us weep with pleasure.
And when our eyes grow blind and death is close
behind,
We shall recite them still whose words our hearts can
fill

With hope beyond all measure.

For God our way, our bread, our rest,
Of all these gifts the Giver.
Our strength, our guide, our nurturing breast
Whose hand will yet deliver.
Who keeps us till the day when night shall
pass away,
When hate and fear are gone and all our work is done,
And we shall sing forever.[8]

Jesus told the story of the Kingdom. A man took out of his treasure something old and something new. Such is the task for those that would make music for the glory of God in our time.

But we must deal with another principle when we consider music in the church.

The Whole Counsel of God

On any given Sunday the whole range of human experience will likely be represented in the church. There will be that widow, trying to hold back the tears, back in church for the first time since her husband died. There is the young man ashamed and embarrassed of his thoughts and feelings. There is a couple whose marriage is unraveling and unsure of what to do. There will be more than one old person there who wonders if life has not passed them by. Someone present may worry about the results of tomorrow's lab report. Another may have lost her job.

Religious music should speak to the whole range of human experience. Paul reminded us that nothing can separate us from the love of God. The great challenge of music in the church is to build a bridge across the chasms of difference and diversity.

In his book, *A Cry of Absence*, church historian Martin Marty says that a mature faith can speak to the full range of the human predicament.[9] He points out that in the

Psalms we find laments, complaints, confessions, questions, prayers of anger as well as adoration, praise, and doxology. Nothing familiar to the human experience of God's children is left out. He says great faith speaks to the wintertime of the soul when the streams are frozen, the ground is hard, and all is cold. That same faith addresses the summertime of life when the skies are blue and everything seems alive. Music in church must run the full gamut if it is to "Speak tenderly to Jerusalem, and cry to her that her warfare is ended, that her iniquity is pardoned, that she has received from the Lord's hand double for all her sins" (Isa. 40:2). The challenge of today's music is to sing the whole counsel of God that all might hear that the news is very good for all who come. This means that we must now consider the controversy between hymns and gospel songs.

Hymns or Gospel Songs

One minister tells of his son going to see the film, *A Trip to Bountiful*. The theme song in that movie was "Softly and Tenderly Jesus Is Calling." Again and again the song is sung and played throughout the movie. The minister's son, graduate of an Ivy League school and frequent church attender, told his father he had never heard that song. He loved the song and was moved by the words and the music. The father confessed that he had made a mistake in ignoring the frontier side of his tradition. Others err by ignoring the great hymns of the church.

The Evangelical tradition should emphasize both gospel songs and hymns. Those of us who are theologically trained forget the primal importance of the songs we sang as little children. The mere singing of "What a Friend We Have in Jesus" or "The Old Rugged Cross" takes us back, back over the years to a special spot some place where our faith journey began. One man with years of education and an important job told his counselor that the only way he could make it some nights was to put the old gospel songs on the stereo and cry himself to sleep.

But every worship leader must be careful lest he give the worshiper only what they ask for. Good taste in the great hymns and anthems can be acquired but it takes time and effort and infinite patience by the worship leader. Part of our task in the church is to raise the sights and standards of those who come. Unless we turn to the hard task of music education little growth will take place. Sydney J. Harris warns us against appealing to the lowest common denominator of people in our churches:

> Popular music changes every few weeks because it is not satisfying; its shallowness soon annoys us. Popular novels must be produced in bulk, because none of them give enough pleasure to last more than one reading. They provide sensation, no nutrition; which is why we call them sensational.
> Bad taste is always changing, because it cannot stand itself. Those who follow their personal preferences soon find they have no preferences except for getting rid of their old ones and finding new ones equally unsatisfying.[10]

The choice for the Evangelical Church is not hymns or gospel songs. The choice is between those things which can enable your people to discover the depth of commitment and love that our faith holds out for all God's children. This means that we must now consider another challenge.

Entertainment or Praise

The church that meets at the end of the 20th century can easily fall into the entertainment trap. People accustomed to being entertained can easily expect to settle into some safe pew as a spectator. Like critics, they go where they find the best show.

The dictionary says that entertainment is defined by passing the time pleasantly, to while away, to divert, please, or amuse. Entertainment does not fit into the biblical understanding of the worship of God. We have already seen that to worship is to see the Lord. To worship is to be jolted out of the everyday experience. Worship means to be changed—inside and out. Worship means, like Isaiah in the Temple, to hear the great voice of the ages and make a response.

The great challenge of worship, then, is to carefully watch the pronouns in music as well as the rest of the service. We are present to glorify God, to find our vision stretched, our lives changed, and our perspectives altered forever. Such an experience is found in the house of the living God when we are lifted out of the role of mere spectators and become participants in the drama of the ages.

Let us now turn to some helpful ways that we can implement the principles we have already discussed.

Singing the Lord's Song

In the average church on Sunday think of the singing you have been involved in. At best there are usually three or four hymns. Some churches include the Doxology, some sing the Gloria Patri or some gospel chorus. But there is a sameness and predictability to most of these services. Let us think of ways that we can involve the whole congregation in greater ways in the music of the church.

Let the congregation be the choir.—This does not mean that we scrap the choir. Far from it. The choir, along with the ministers, are worship leaders for the congregation. I propose that we enlarge the circle and bring the full congregation into a greater singing role in the church.

Let the people sing the call to worship. What better way for the people of God to begin worship than to lift up their longings for the day in a choral call to worship that

all sing. The key to such innovation will be the familiarity
of the people. Nothing stifles worship like beginning on a
note of the unfamiliar. Begin prayerfully and quietly by
singing together: "We Are Climbing Jacob's Ladder."
You might begin by singing: "Kum Bah Yah" or the familiar: "Spirit of the Living God." Select the call to worship to fit the mood and spirit of the service and let the
people sing.

Let the people sing the prayer responses. With a little
training and explanation before the service this might be
a meaningful innovation. "Hear Our Prayer, O Lord" is a
possibility. Another prayer response might be Ken Medema's, "Lord, Listen to Your Children Praying." The
chorus of "There Is a Balm in Gilead" provides a beautiful way to respond to the invocation.

Let the people sing after the Scripture reading. A wonderful way to punctuate the power of the Word of God is
for people to sing a response. You might use "Wonderful
Words of Life," the chorus to Fosdick's hymn, "Grant us
wisdom, grant us courage for the living of these days." A
prayerful singing of "Break Thou the Bread of Life," may
prove meaningful.

Let the people sing after candidates are baptized.
English Baptists have been doing this for years. As the
candidate comes out of the water, the congregation
breaks into song. Sometimes they might sing the " Doxology," a stanza of "Amazing Grace," or the chorus of "O
Happy Day that Fixed My Choice" ("Happy day, happy
day, when Jesus washed my sins away . . ."). The chorus of
the familiar: "At the Cross" might be a possibility.

Let the people sing their confessions. One of the most
powerful movements that many have discovered in worship is the confession time just before the taking of the
Lord's Supper. A new hymn which helps the people prepare for the Supper is set to the tune of "Jacob's Ladder."

O Lord Jesus, cast our sin out.
Lord, have mercy; Christ, have mercy.
Take away our life of sin now.
Jesus, hear our prayer.

Fill our empty lives with your love.
Give our lives some great new purpose.
Send your Spirit to live in us.
Jesus, hear our prayer.

You, alone, Lord, can transform us.
You, alone, can we depend on.
You, alone, can give us power.
Jesus, hear our prayer.

Glory to God, peace to all men.
Let us praise him, let us bless him.
Let us give our lives to serve him.
Jesus, hear our prayer. Amen.[11]

When the elements of the Lord's Supper are passed becomes a great time for the people to respond in singing. As the bread is passed you might sing one song. You might select another appropriate hymn during the passing of the cup.

Let the people sing in response to the gifts of the day. The receiving of the gifts becomes a time when all can sing. Many churches have been singing the " Doxology" for years and this is meaningful. On some Sundays vary this practice. Sing one stanza of "Now Thank We All Our God." On World Hunger Sunday you might sing, "Someone's Hungry Lord, Come by Here." At Christmastime you might use a stanza of "Joy to the World" after the offering throughout the Christmas season.

Let the people sing the benedictions. The ending of the service is a great time to focus again on the theme of the service. Some Sunday you might use one stanza of the chorus: "We Shall Be as One" and use the last stanza of that chorus at the benediction time. Some churches end the service with "Blest Be the Tie that Binds." and others sing: "We Are One in the Bond of Love." Variety lifts the people out of their lethargy and brings the gospel into play in fresh ways. You might end by singing, "They'll Know We Are Christians By Our Love."

These are only suggestions. The possibilities are endless once you begin to see that the whole hymnal and musical repertoire of your people offer new possibilities for the worship of God. Like our Baptist ancestors, let us return to the principle of creating new ways for our people to worship. One does not have to do something different every week, but occasionally change will help your people see God in a way they have not seen Him before.

Weave the whole service around a musical theme.—On the Sunday nearest July Fourth use patriotic hymns throughout the service, even the invitation. For a sermon on the Lord's Prayer work with your minister of music to use a variety of musical pieces around this beautiful Psalm. One Christmas I chose music from Handel's *Messiah* and blended pieces of that great music with a exposition of Isaiah 40.[12] The same format could be used for the Lenten portion of the *Messiah* and selected passages of Scripture. One Sunday you might devote to Isaac Watts, preach a biographical sermon on the hymnodist, and use some of the great Watts' music exclusively throughout the service. Another Sunday you might turn to Johann Bach, Fanny Crosby, or B. B. McKinney. Why not take a Race Relations Sunday and sing only Negro spirituals as the sermon talks about how music has helped black people through the years? Focus on their contribution to our cultural and religious heritage.

Rediscover the hymnal.—The church lives by two basic books: the Bible and the hymnal. The Bible records God's revelation to his people; the hymnal focuses on our response to God.[13] Just as many ministers err in ignoring

large passages of the Bible, many churches have neglected many hymns in our hymnals. Teach the people about
the index, about the history of the great hymns of the
faith, use illustrations from how our hymns came to be.
Some of the richest illustrations are neglected and they
come from some of the most familiar hymns in our book.[14]
When Robert Ingersoll, the famous atheist of the 19th
century died, the Boston paper carried a lengthy article
on his life and death and the funeral service. The last
lines describing the funeral service are telling. The obitu-
ary ended: "There was no music." In the life of faith music flows like a river, helping the people of God sing their
praises to Almighty God whatever the condition of their
lives.

Notes

1. Garrison Keillor, *Lake Wobegon Days* (New York: Viking Pen-
quin, 1985), 217-218. Used by permission.
2. E. Werner, "Music," in *The Interpreter's Dictionary of the Bible*,
vol. K-Q, George A. Buttrick, Editor (Nashville: Abingdon, 1962), 457-
469.
3. Thomas R. McKibbens, "Our Baptist Heritage in Worship,"
quoted in *The Review and Expositor*, Southern Baptist Theological
Seminary, Louisville, Kentucky, Winter, 1983, 59.
4. *Ibid.*
5. Dan Wakefield, *Returning* (New York: Doubleday, 1988), 16.
Used by permission.
6. Robert D. Dale, *To Dream Again* (Nashville: Broadman, 1981),
54-55.
7. "We Shall Be As One," published in *Songs of Fellowship*, Book
One (Eastbourne, E. Sussex: Kingsway Publications, LTD, 1984), p.
150, Copyright © 1978, Thankyou Music, P.O. Box 75, Eastbourne
BN23 6NW.
8. Ken Medema has given permission to use this hymn text. He
suggests any church can use his text when they give appropriate
credit.
9. Martin Marty, *A Cry of Absence* (San Francisco: Harper & Row,
Publishers, 1983), 132.

10. Quoted in Paul W. Wohlgemuth, *Rethinking Church Music* (Carol Stream, Illinois: Hope Publishing Company, 1981), 18.

11. *Ventures in Worship*, Edited by David James Randolph (Nashville: Abingdon Press, 1969), 87.

12. Roger Lovette, "Blending the Messiah with the Gospel Message," in *Proclaim*, October-December, 1985, 6-13.

13. Dale, 55.

14. Two excellent sources to help you find the stories behind the hymns are: Albert Edward Bailey's, *The Gospel in Hymns* (New York: Charles Scribner's Sons, 1950), and William J. Reynolds' *Companion to Baptist Hymnal* (Nashville: Broadman Press, 1976).

5

Rabbits and Jesus

When the disciples, overearnest as ever, asked Jesus who was the greatest in the kingdom of Heaven, Jesus pulled a child out of the crowd and said the greatest in the kingdom of Heaven were people like this . . . Two thousand years of homiletic sentimentalizing to the contrary notwithstanding, Jesus was not playing Captain Kangaroo. He was saying that the people who get into Heaven are people who, like children, don't worry about it too much. They are people who, like children, live with their hands open more than with their fists clenched. They are people who, like children, are so relatively unburdened by preconceptions that if somebody says there's a pot of gold at the end of the rainbow, they are perfectly willing to go take a look for themselves. Children aren't necessarily better than other people. Like the child in "The Emperor's New Clothes," they are just apt to be better at telling the difference between a put-up job and the real thing.

—Frederick Buechner[1]

Truly, I say to you, unless you turn and become like children, you will never enter the kingdom of heaven (Matt. 18:3).

During a children's sermon the minister held up a picture of a rabbit. He asked the boys and girls who squirmed at the front of the church if they knew what was in the picture. After a long pause, one little boy

raised his hand, "It looks like a rabbit, but I know I'm
supposed to say Jesus."

It is no wonder that many churches view children's sermons with great suspicion. And it is no surprise that
many churches have tried this new addition to their worship only to scrap it. This part of the service easily falls
into moralizing, into demeaning the minds of little children, and holds out a theology that can easily be mindless
and unreal. Buechner is right. This is not Captain Kangaroo time in worship. The children's time ought to provide
children and adults with an experience like that day our
Lord lifted a child high above the disciples' heads and
made the child feel special and important. No wonder
children flocked to Jesus. He gave them a dignity and a
joy that they found few places in their lives. The worship
leader who follows biblical principles, sound developmen-
tal psychology, and common sense might just find the circle of worship growing larger and wider until it takes in
even the little ones that come Sunday after Sunday.

A seminary professor once said that if you want to
know something about the depth of a pastor's ministry,
watch how the children respond to that minister. These
words have haunted me for years.

Sunday after Sunday I watched the children scribble
away during the morning worship service. I noticed their
restlessness, their whisperings, and their parents' desperate attempts to keep them from disturbing those around
them. They seemed to be cut off from the worship service,
wishing to be anywhere else.

Dave Holmes has written creatively about children's
worship. He has said that if any adult wonders what it is
like to be a small child in worship take a piece of string
about a yard long, cross your ankles together and tie your
feet together. Then tell the adult there is to be no talking
whatsoever. Next he asks the adults to sit on their hands.
While their feet are tied, their mouths are clamped shut

and they are sitting on their hands, Holmes says the minister should talk and talk and talk.[2] Much of worship is like this to the small child. It is senseless to the children and the energy and exuberance of the little ones is so constrained that they only feel miserable.

During a revival which I conducted in another town I decided to use a part of the service every evening especially for the children. I encouraged all the little ones of the congregation to come down to the front of the church. Then I used an object lesson to explain a particular facet of the Christian faith. There was a lot of dialogue and participation. The children seemed to enjoy this part of the service and I enjoyed talking to them night after night. After I returned home I decided to try this same approach in the church I served.

That experience happened over 20 years ago. And since that time there has been a spot in our service for children. From the very beginning I was surprised at the response of my own children. Very soon they were looking forward to this part of our worship. Parents started calling me to tell how much their children enjoyed the worship service. Older adults would whisper that the children's time was becoming their favorite part of the service. I have been rewarded many times after the service when our little ones have stopped to tell me something special or to hand me some love gift of their scribblings—sometimes meticulously folded in an offering envelope. On occasions they have just stopped by to give their pastor a great big kiss.

The children's sermon is now a vital part of our morning worship service. As soon as the Doxology is sung and the offertory prayer is said, I step down from the pulpit and invite the children to come forward and sit with me on the steps. From all over the sanctuary they stream forward for "their time." Some churches have the organist play "Jesus Loves Me" as they come forward. We use these moments as the children come forward for adults to greet one another during the service.

How Children Learn

As the children find their places at the front of the
church it is important for the person doing the children's
sermon to understand something of how children learn.
One of the great mistakes we make is paring down some
biblical truth that completely flies over the heads of the
children.

We have learned a great deal the last few years about
how children learn. Religious educators tell us that:

Children learn 10 percent of what they hear; 30 percent
of what they see; 60 percent of what they do.[3] The more
the children are engaged in a learning experience the
greater their chances that they will remember what they
have heard. What they have been told may not stick at
all. Yet we know that when they learn to ride a bicycle it
stays with them because total participation is demanded
of the learner.

One of the first rules in doing the children's sermon is
that: "Thou shalt not talk excessively." In their early
years they are discovering reality through their senses—
seeing, touching, tasting, and feeling. Consequently those
giving children's sermons need to rely on whatever resources are available to engage the child in learning. Abstract stories and principles must be filtered through the
senses.[4]

One mistake that we often make in talking to children
is in making our subject too complicated. We bring in too
many issues and ideas. For years we have been told that
the sermon should have one point. Sharpen your message
until you have one central point that the children can
take home. Challenge them to participate, to let their creativity run wild. Implement sound educational principles
and the gospel will come alive for the little ones in your
church.

One Sunday I told the children that we were going to take a trip. And I asked them to follow me. We walked up the aisle of the church until we found a couple that were celebrating their 50th anniversary that day. I stopped at their pew and asked the couple to stand. I asked them where they got married and asked them to tell about their wedding. Then I asked the children and the congregation to lead us in singing "Happy Anniversary" to them. The children learned something about the Christian understanding of fidelity in marriage, they participated in community, and they graced an elderly couple who had been married for 50 years.

Another Sunday we talked about world hunger in church. That morning I pulled a candy bar from my pocket. I gave each child a tiny piece of the candy. Then I gave one of the children three-fourths of the candy bar. I asked the child to eat the candy bar while the others watched. Then I talked to them about how they felt about this experience. I finished with Jesus' words in Matthew 25 about feeding the hungry.

Simply to call the children to the front and drone on and one about any subject misses the children entirely. Study carefully how children learn and you will help your children and adults enormously.

One of the criticisms that many make of this time in the service is that what is said is so superficial and theologically bland that many pastors leave out the children's time entirely. Every part of worship should flow from a sound theological base, and this is certainly true with the children.

What Are We to Teach?

God.—Theology begins with God, whether we are working with children or adults. Unless we can enlarge a child's capacity for love of God we have missed the point. Children are naturally inquisitive and this gives us a great opportunity to teach them some substantive things about their Heavenly Father.

We begin by teaching them that God is Father. This is not easy. For fatherhood is a poor model for children in our times. Many of those sitting so piously at the front are from broken homes and only see their fathers on weekends and special days. Many live with stepfathers. Others see their busy fathers infrequently. But we start with God as a good Father.

You might begin with a picture of the prodigal son. Bernand's, *Der Verlorme Sohn,* is a powerful picture of an old man with his arms around his barefooted son. He took the boy back after he had done many terrible things. You might give them copies of the picture and tell them to look at that picture every night before they go to sleep.

One Sunday you might tell the story of that time in the Temple when Jesus lifted a child and talked about how He loved him. You might pass out copies of the familiar Sunday School picture of Jesus, friend of children. Such images give them some understanding that words can never do.

One rule of thumb is to make sure you do not give the child some picture of God that must be unlearned later. Poor pictures of God are not easily forgotten. Anyone who has had the experience of learning to hunt and peck on a typewriter and then having to unlearn that experience in a typing course knows the difficulty of such an assignment. Teach them pictures of God they can live with all their lives and you will have given them a great gift.

Self.—One of the things that children need to learn from church is acceptance and forgiveness. Very early they are programmed to feel that they are not very important in the scheme of things. They are tiny people in an adult world. The good news tells them they are to love their neighbors as they *love themselves.* We must not

obliterate that great vision that Jesus gave us when He
held a child in His arms.

If children's sermons can make children feel good
about themselves they will respond in positive ways. One
Sunday I came in with a suitcase filled with clothing.
Sweaters and pants and jackets and hats and gloves—
there were many items in that suitcase. Then I asked one
child to put on everything I had in that suitcase. The child
could hardly move. Then I told Ken Medema's story of
how a little boy or girl hated themselves and thought they
were ugly. So they put on layer after layer of clothing
hoping to cover up who they were. But the gospel says
that He loves us just like we are. After asking the child to
walk around, which was difficult, I asked the child to begin to take off the excess clothing and put it back in the
suitcase. She discovered she could walk and run and felt
much more comfortable. I told them that God loved them
just as they were.

Another Sunday I asked them what they hated about
themselves. Some said they were too fat, too short, their
ears were too big, they didn't like their noses. Some said
they weren't good at sports or games. I asked them to look
at the adults. Did anyone there have a big nose? Were any
of them short? Did they think the adults liked everything
about themselves? And then I asked if they thought God
loved the adults in the house. I ended that message by
saying that God loves us all just like we are. One Sunday
we ended that message with the choir singing Ken Medema's chorus "Did You Know That You're a Person, ...
That You're OK."[5]

Others.—Another important theological lesson that
children need to learn in church is that they live in a
world with other people. They are tied to others, and they
must get along with others. Not only must they love
themselves, they must also love their neighbors.

Role playing is a way to involve the children in the message of the gospel. Why not act out the story of the good Samaritan one Sunday and teach them that they are to be kind and respond to others in need?

World need.—Children in an affluent society need to be exposed to human need. They need to hear that part of the gospel that says "to whom much is given, much shall be required." Missions and social problems can be dealt with at this time of the service. During the foreign missions emphasis why not introduce the visiting missionary to the children and let the missionary tell a little about the work. The missionary might explain how important it is for all God's children to share the good news by giving to missions.

One Sunday I took one of Walter's Keane's pictures of a little ragged girl with the big eyes and passed it around for the children to see. I asked them how they felt about the child in the picture. I asked them if they had ever seen any child with sad eyes. Then I asked them if Jesus did not want us to help those sad-eyed children all over the world. We bowed our heads and prayed for children everywhere.

The children's time is a great opportunity to involve the children in worship. This teaching does not have to be left to the minister or the church staff. In every church there is a core of talented laypersons who love children and can communicate the great ideas of the Christian faith to them. Use their gifts and the circle of worship leadership will grow wider.

A Word of Warning

Children's time in worship is only one of many ways in which we are to draw our young into the circle of participation. To limit communication to the children to only one special time can be mere tokenism. This moment in the service should be only one way of making sure your children are included in the worship experience.

Older children can light candles on special occasions like Advent. They might serve as junior ushers from time to time. With some training they could give out bulletins and take up the collection.

As you prepare your worship services, plan with the children in mind. Sing a hymn occasionally which the children will know. Select illustrations in your sermons that children can understand and identify with. If you have a junior church program you might have your leaders to teach the children the Lord's Prayer and some of the hymns that adults sing. A careful teaching program on the different dimensions of worship will help them understand your church's worship. Occasionally have the children's choirs to sing in church. If Jesus was right, planning for children in our services Sunday after Sunday is important.[6]

However you incorporate children into your service, make sure that you remember that beautiful picture of Jesus standing in the Temple with a child in His arms. Such a vision will challenge you to seek new ways to make worship meaningful to the little ones in your congregation.

Notes

1. Frederick Buechner, *Wishful Thinking* (New York: Harper & Row Publishers, 1973), 13.

2. Dave Holmes, *Involving the Little Person in Worship,* part II, was privately printed and can be ordered from Dave Holmes, 402 So. Carroll, Rock Rapids, Iowa 51246.

3. Richard Coleman, *Gospel Telling* (Grand Rapids, Michigan: Eerdman), 16.

4. Richard Coleman, in *Gospel Telling,* suggests two excellent books

which can teach us much about how children and adults learn. Thomas Groome, *Christian Religious Education: Sharing Our Story and Vision* (San Francisco: Harper & Row, 1981). Two other books which I have found helpful are: William Hendricks, *A Theology for Children* (Nashville: Broadman Press, 1980) and James Fowler's *Stages of Faith* (San Francisco: Harper & Row, 1981).

5. Ken Medema, recording. "Ken Medema and Friends: Just Us Kids," (Waco, Texas: Word Records, 1976).

6. Dave Holmes has some excellent suggestions of different ways to involve children in the worship service on page 6 of his unpublished manuscript.

6

How Can Man Preach?

Lord, how can man preach thy eternall word?
He is a brittle crazie glasse:
Yet in thy temple thou dost him afford
This glorious and transcendent place,
To be a window, through thy grace.
—George Herbert[1]

Now after John was arrested, Jesus came into
Galilee, preaching the gospel of God, and saying,
"The time is fulfilled, and the kingdom of God is at
hand; repent, and believe in the gospel" (Mark 1:14-
15).

At the very center of our worship we find a pulpit. And
at midpoint in almost every service there will be a sermon. Preaching has always occupied a prominent place
in the Evangelical Church. People come back Sunday after Sunday expecting to hear some word from the Lord.

To understand the prominence of this act we must begin with the source. It is a long, winding journey from the
place where we preach to that spot, years ago, where it all
started.

The church, in recalling that beginning, remembered it
as an ordinary day. So commonplace that many must
have stayed home and slept late. As ordinary as those
days when we would give almost anything to be somewhere else. But that morning the Healer had come back

home. Maybe to see His family. Perhaps He came to touch
the base once more, to retrace the familiar haunts of His
early days. Luke said, "as his custom was"(4:16). He
walked down the dusty road with His brothers and sisters
to the synagogue. He sat down with people He had known
all His life.

They asked Him to read that day. Maybe because the
hometown boy had made good, maybe because no one else
there could read—or would. Things grew quiet as He
agreed to read. Someone coughed. A mother pulled a little one close and whispered that he must be still. A young
Jewish boy looked across the aisle at a beautiful Jewish
girl. She smiled back. Jesus made His way through the
crowd, looking at people whose faces He knew. He picked
up the old Isaiah scroll. He carefully unrolled it and began to read. And this is the source. Here we find the beginning of the sermon.

What did Jesus read? And what did He say that day?
Luke said He read the words that were already engraved
on His heart. He must have learned them as a boy. That
Scripture passage gives us a clue for all that will follow:

> The Spirit of the Lord is upon me, because he hath
> anointed me to preach the gospel to the poor, he hath
> sent me to heal the brokenhearted, to preach deliver-
> ance to the captives, and recovering of sight to the
> blind, to set at liberty them that are bruised, To
> preach the acceptable year of the Lord (Luke 4:18-19,
> KJV)

The church remembered that, after He read those
words, He rolled the scroll back up and gave it to the leader in charge and sat down. From His pew He preached the
sermon. All He would ever say flowed out of that tiny riv-
ulet that can be traced back to Isaiah 61.

Legend has it that the evangelist Billy Sunday always
opened his Bible to Isaiah 61 when he preached. *"The*

Spirit of the Lord is upon me, because he hath anointed me to preach the gospel to the poor. . . . " Billy would leave his notes resting on this magnificent text. One wonders if Billy, in his crazy, wild flamboyance, looking down on his tattered notes, spread out on the afflictions and brokenness and captives—did not see what Isaiah and Jesus saw.

The preacher today stumbles into the house Sunday after plodding Sunday. He hopes that the foolishness of his preaching may just reach his own heart and then move across the pews back there to the shadows where someone sits in quiet desperation. Like Isaiah and Jesus and even Billy Sunday and all the rest who have dared to preach— what the preacher thinks or says must rest solidly on those words that Jesus read that morning in Nazareth. This is the source.

What do we find, embedded, in those words that can add vitality and meaning to our preaching today?

A Good Model

When we think of those early preachers, our minds turn to Peter who had such success on the Day of Pentecost. Or we remember Paul taking on the pagans on Mars Hill. The word *preacher* evokes images like Mark, Doctor Luke, or John the Baptist with all his wildness and power. To these we may add those preachers through the ages who have moved so many. None of these become our primary model. Dr. Buttrick understood this in his Lyman Beecher Lectures when he called them, *Jesus Came Preaching.* The Lord is our model and our great mentor for preaching.

What can the preacher learn from Jesus as a model? Rollo May, in *Courage to Create,* tells of an artist who, after his death, left one final canvas as his last will and testament. At first glance the painting seemed to be empty. But right in the middle of all that whitened space there was one word faintly written. Some thought the word was *solitude,* others said it read *solidarity.* Rollo May states that any creativity must embody not one of these words but both. Creativity flows from solitude and solidarity.[2] We are fed by being alone and fed by the marketplace with the noises of life all around us.

Jesus' life ran like a shuttle between solitude and solidarity. Those who knew Him best saw the light of the Lord's face shining through all He did. And so they begged Him to teach them to pray.

Later, when he left the mount of transfiguration He found those that He had taught to pray powerless and in despair. A child convulsed. His followers did not know what to do. Later, after He had healed the child and the crowd had scattered, He whispered the secret of His power. "This kind cannot be driven out by anything but prayer"Mark 9:29).

Solitude means time with the Bible and books and even time away from work. Three years ago the church I served granted me a two-month sabbatical in England. I took only two books with me, the Bible and Walter Brueggemann's commentary on *Genesis.* While I was in England on that pulpit exchange, I preached old sermons. I studied little. I reveled in the time with my family, in discovering new places and meeting new friends. For two months my mind lay fallow. I was afraid when autumn and responsibility returned I would have nothing to say. But, on returning, I discovered the well of creativity which I thought was empty filled up and ran over. I began preaching again on Genesis 1—11 and the texts came alive everywhere I turned. This gift of time was the church's greatest gift to me, and mine, in turn, to them. There is no creativity without solitude.

But the reverse is also true. There is no creativity without solidarity—living in the marketplace. For the Scottish congregation was right when they spoke of their pastor. He was invisible during the week and incomprehensible on Sunday.

Several years ago Baptists lost one of their great voices when L. D. Johnson died. Like many others I attended his funeral on a cold December afternoon. The large church was packed that day. *The Greenville News* had written of him that morning, "Greenville has lost its conscience." Looking around the church there were governors, senators, domestics, and little girls and boys he had baptized. There were students and preachers from all over. The pastor summarized that occasion by quoting from the memorial service of Sir Christopher Wren, the great London architect. "If you would see the man's monuments, look around." Dr. Johnson loved people and they knew it. His compassion came from the Source—the One who had been friend of publicans and sinners.

The preacher takes his clue from Jesus. Our Lord spoke to those that He knew well. These were no strangers. He was well-acquainted with the betrayer, the doubter, those who jockeyed for power, the deceiver, the anxious, the self-confident, and the lonely. He was acquainted with their griefs because He was one with them.

The preacher will find no creativity in isolation from his world. Next week as you begin your sermon preparation write down in the margin of your notes the people in your church with real needs. Here is my list:

Jim has just lost his wife of 61 years. His son had a stroke the week after the funeral and Jim lost his brother the same week. Since that time he has had prostrate surgery and discovered he has leukemia.

Melba's mother is dying of lupus and they just

moved her into a nursing home because they know
she needs constant care.

Terry and Linda sit there scared. Just this week
they found out they have lost their business, and
they do not know if they can even save their home.

Doug always sits on the right side in church. Tomorrow he goes to Duke hospital for another round
of chemotherapy. He is 32, just finished a Ph.D. and
worries about his wife and three children.

Martha's husband sits on the back row. She can't
come because her rheumatoid arthritis is too bad,
and she must have another round of surgery on her
feet soon.

Hank sits across the aisle on the back row, too. His
wife died suddenly and he married too hastily and
that marriage is not working out. He does not know
what to do.

Becky will not be here today and neither will her
husband, but their two teenagers came. She is fed up
with being married and has asked her husband for a
divorce.

Mike is not here today and neither is his mother or
sister. In the North-South game as our best quarter-
back he broke his ankle in a terrible fracture. The
schools that have courted him for years have quit
calling. He sits at home, staring out the window. Tomorrow he will begin relearning how to walk on that
broken ankle.

The pastor who knows and loves his people will speak a
good word from the Lord when he stands to preach. And
those who come will listen carefully. Like those who first
heard Jesus' words, they will discover something that can

take them through whatever they face.

A Good Foundation

The creative preacher will also build his sermon on a rock that has stood the test of time. Jesus provides our model for that foundation.

Jesus rested His case on that bedrock of Scripture He had learned as a boy. This was His authority as He spoke that first day in the synagogue.

He spoke with power because he had woven the words of Isaiah 61 into His own heart and life. Only days before, when He was tempted He had fallen back on the Book of Deuteronomy. Later, when He breathed His last, He would reach back to those words His mother had taught Him from the Psalter: "Father, into thy hands I commend my spirit" (Luke 34:46, KJV).

The great danger of so much of our preaching is that in the busyness of so many demands the preacher touches lightly the text and it touches lightly the people and it touches the preacher lightly, too, if at all. There is a destitution in churches across this land. Like those days long ago, "And the word of the Lord was rare in those days; there was no frequent vision" (1 Sam.3:1).

We must return to the Scriptures. Biblical exposition is hard work, but those who do it will find an authority in their preaching that was not there before. They will find their lives changed and they will speak to a people hungry for a word that can only come from the Lord. Like our Master, we are to be servants of the Word.

Our message, resting on this solid foundation, will not fall away to the heresies that blow in our time. For the preacher will find his or her life changed and preaching will take on a new vitality. For those who unwrap the old scroll, read the words and ponder deep the message will discover the old miracle breaking loose in their lives and

in those around them. "Today this scripture has been fulfilled in your hearing" (Luke 4:21).

A Great Theme

Years ago, as a young, green, 25-year-old seminary
graduate in my first church, I was having a hard time as
pastor. So one night I drove across the county to hear the
great Ralph Sockman preach. I was electrified by the sermon and can still remember many of the things he said
that evening. After the service I made my way through
the crowd to speak to the great man. I found him gracious, approachable, and very kind. When I asked him the
secret of his sermons, he told me, "Young man, preach on
the great themes and you will never go wrong." Dr. Sockman had learned that lesson from the Source. Jesus never
dealt with the inconsequentials of life. He was heard and
followed because the great themes He chose spoke to the
places of the heart.

Luke recorded, as prelude, there at the beginning of
Jesus' ministry, what He would do. He reached back to
Isaiah and the Exile to undergird all He would say. Jesus
brought good news and tidings of great joy. He painted on
a large canvas. This was His message in Nazareth.

Good news to the poor.—The pastor in every age must
begin with the dispossessed. Some time ago I spoke to an
ethics class at a denominational university. The class was
filled with Christian students who had been on mission
trips to California, Europe, and Florida. I began by asking
them how many of them knew the names of the maids
who swept the floor. They stared blankly at me. One of
those women had been working there for 25 years. Not a
single one of those students had even looked at those custodians. The last parable our Lord gave, may have been
partial repayment of an old debt whose theme began in
Luke 4: "Inasmuch as ye have done it unto the least of

these my brethren, ye have done it unto me" (Matt.25:40, KJV).

Healing for the brokenhearted.—This term is no slight disappointment. For the word *brokenhearted* means a complete disintegration, a breaking into pieces. Sometimes this brokenness is spiritual, and often it is physical.

Like the late anthropologist, Loren Eiseley, we who preach are to be students of broken things. This subject has been dealt with at length in Dr. James Lynch's, *The Broken Heart.* His book deals with the medical consequences of loneliness. His main thesis is that the number-one killer in America is heart disease. And Dr. Lynch believes that we have spent far too much time on scientific and technical causes of the disease. He states bluntly that we may shorten our own lives by the lack of human companionship. Our hearts break because we have few strong ties to other people. His list of victims of congestive heart failure could provide any preacher with themes for a lifetime.

1. Death by a relative
2. Relatives' refusal to care for her
3. Sudden death of a son
4. Desertion of one son and landlady; serious accident to other son
5. Illness of mother; argument with wife
6. Desertion by wife
7. Sudden death of husband
8. Husband's death—rejection by relatives
9. Rejection by husband and son
10. Marriage of daughter; wife's leg amputated
11. Desertion by husband
12. Rejection by children
13. Desertion by brother and sister-in-law
14. Rejection by employer
15. Rejection by husband
16. Eviction from home of 18 years

17. Eviction from home of 17 years
18. Loss of pseudomasculine defenses[3]

Alongside these we might well place Emily Dickinson's longing as the preacher's own charge:

> If I could stop one Heart from breaking
> I shall not live in vain
> If I can ease one Life the Aching
> Or cool one Pain
>
> Or help one fainting Robin
> Unto his Nest again
> I shall not live in Vain.[4]

Real preaching must give serious attention to the brokenhearted.

Deliverance to the captives.—After the exiles were released from bondage they discovered to their horror that the work was not over. They faced a broken land, loss of will, an eroding faith, and weariness everywhere. When Jesus looked out that morning in His hometown it was no different. Looking into faces He had known all His life, He saw a sea of captivity all over that room: Jews held captive by Rome; old men held captive by a hundred different chains; women held captive by a culture that treated them as less than cattle; children limping through life and dying before their time, captive to ignorance, sin, and injustice.

The church today must, in Merrill Abbey's splendid term, challenge the axioms of our time. What are some of our modern axioms?

> Our overemphasis on the physical;
> The Success Syndrome;
> The "Me and My" decade;
> Winning through intimidation;
> The Super-Bowl mentality;

Greed, selfishness, and materialism.

The captives have yet to be delivered.

To recover sight to the blind.—Blindness was an obsession in the Old Testament. It was everywhere. And Jesus picked up the theme again when he continually said, "Look, see, open your eyes!"

Today's preacher has the very large task of forcing his or her people to, as Annie Dillard says, "explore the neighborhood." For the lens through which we view life determines what we see. One of the reasons there may be so few Pauls today may be because there are still so few Ananiases. The blind still need a touch and a whisper that says "Brother or Sister." Only then will the scales fall off. The words, *born again* or *conversion*, were once very large words. They turned one inside out. Everything was changed. We are still charged to bring sight to the blind.

To give liberty to the bruised.—Recently Americans contributed millions of dollars to give the Statue of Liberty a new face-lift. This symbol of hope for millions of immigrants was rededicated in a glorious Fourth Of July celebration. But the symbol will prove meaningless if the people that come to live in this new land do not find what the creators of the statue had in mind years ago. "Give me your tired, your poor, . . . the homeless. . . . "

We are to restore liberty to the bruised. All those victimized by our time look to the church for help. Little children in Third-World countries live from cradle to grave scared of bombs, violence, and disruption. Christian teachers often prefer teaching the smart kids in public school instead of the disadvantaged. Who will give freedom and liberty to all who cannot speak for themselves?

So the task of the sermon, the preacher, and the church is to proclaim in all they do that this is the year of the

Lord's favor. This is the great occasion when the Lord's lovingkindness will arrive, not just for the privileged, but for all. Those preachers who return to this great Source will find that the river of God is full of water. That living water is adequate for every need.

A Proper Context

Jesus delivered that first sermon in the synagogue. Creative preaching does not take place in isolation. It arises out of a worship setting. Preaching never stands alone.

For too long the Evangelical Church made the sermon everything. But historically, great preaching has been set in the golden frame of Christian worship. Jesus went to the synagogue "as his custom was" (Luke 4:16). Jesus brought the struggles of His own life to the synagogue, surrounded by the familiar words and hymns from the Psalter and the prayers of the community of the faithful.

This whole volume underlines the setting of the sermon. Creative worship does not take away from the sermon, but undergirds and strengthens the message. Those services that are planned, worked on, prayed down, and participatory in nature will change, renew, enable, and strengthen the lives of those who come.

In another part of this book I will deal with the importance of the nonverbal symbols in worship. The great danger of our tradition has been in its peculiar reliance on the verbal symbol to carry the whole of the gospel story. This is simply not possible.

Years ago, as a young college student, I spent a summer working out West. I had never seen mountains like the Wasatch range in Utah. I stared at those peaks and reveled in their beauty. I took photograph after photograph trying to capture the majesty of that mountain range. When I returned home I discovered none of my slides did the mountains justice. I had bits of pieces of that wonder to remember. The mountains were too large and too great

to be captured by any photograph. Our encounters with
God are like that. Nothing can do justice to His majesty.
Surely words alone cannot touch the wonder. We may
need all our resources to begin to express something of
the holy at the heart of life.

Out of the context of His own tradition, Jesus spoke a
healing word. The preacher who sanctifies his or her
imagination will use all the senses, architecture, and all
the church's traditions to speak a good word for Jesus
Christ. Creative preaching is set down in the midst of the
agony and ecstasy of the people's life and work.

A Risky Business

Those who return to the Source of our preaching must
read the story all the way to the end. After Jesus' sermon
Luke gave us the people's response: "When they heard
this, all in the synagogue were filled with wrath. And
they rose up and put him out of the city, and led him to
the brow of the hill on which their city was built, that
they might throw him down headlong" (Luke 4:28-29).
For Luke this was merely a foreshadowing of all that
would follow. Three years later we remember how it ended on Calvary's hill.

Creative preaching is risky business. Risk and courage
are required of the faithful preacher in any age. Wallace
Fisher has written:

> The radical difference between twentieth-century
> preaching and first-century preaching comes into
> sharp focus when the diplomatic ways of many con-
> temporary preachers are compared with the bold
> thrusts of those first-century preachers—Peter,
> Paul, and Stephen. The former are elected to service
> clubs; the latter were arrested for disturbing the
> peace, run out of town, or murdered. Contrast the ca-
> sual congregational response to much contemporary

preaching with the concerned, angry, violent response to the preaching of those men. Peter's congregation, cut to the heart, cried out, "What shall we do
to be saved?" Paul's message so infuriated the silver-
smiths in Ephesus that he had to leave town. Stephen's forthright preaching led to his murder.[5]

Those that hug the shoreline and cling to the old safe-
ties will never preach creatively to their congregations.
The Word of God cuts like a sharp two-edged sword. Real
preaching demands risk.

Walter Brueggemann has pointed out that in the Old
Testament there was an incalculable tension between
Temple and Torah. The Temple represented safety, the
settled, and the guaranteed. So the Temple was their
sanctuary—a place to hide from the storms. But Brueggemann says this was only part of the Old Testament story.
There towered above the people the Torah. And the Torah was obedience to God's teachings, God's way, and
God's will.[5] Good preaching must, by its very nature,
stretch us to confrontation, to change, to a faith which
takes us down roads we have never been before. This is a
risky business indeed.

Our Evangelical tradition is a risky tradition. That little band of believers led by John Smyth were driven from
place to place because of an undaunted message they
would not give up. John Bunyan was jailed for years because of his preaching. The jails of Virginia were full and
running over with Baptist preachers who refused to keep
silent. Walter Rauschenbusch raised his voice over the
ghettos in New York; Martin Luther King died for his
dream.

T.S. Eliot captured the riskiness of such a faith when he
wrote:

> Remember the faith that took men from home
> At the call of a wandering preacher.

Our age is an age of moderate virtue
And moderate vice
When men will not lay down the Cross
Because they will never assume it.
Yet nothing is impossible, nothing,
To men of faith and conviction.[7]

And then Eliot added:

Let us therefore make perfect our will.
O God, help us.[8]

Only in the risking do we stretch and only in the stretching do we discover something of the full measure of the gifts that Christ Jesus holds out for us all.

A Connecting Link

Jesus' sermon in His hometown might never have been remembered without the connecting link. He told the story of Elijah and the lepers and the Syrian Namaan and linked that story to the condition of His hearers in Nazareth. If Jesus had only told the story, little would have happened. But our Lord made the application to their lives and their time and the Word of God began to do its painful work.

Any real gospel makes the connections between the biblical truth and the cultural context of our lives. Without these ties the gospel becomes vague and irrelevant. Halford Luccock understood this when he wrote:

It is when we move the good Samaritan from the Jericho Road to Main Street, just around the corner, or move the rich fool from Judea to our neighborhood in Nebraska or Texas, or move Judas into our own congregation, that the trouble begins; and that is when real preaching begins.[9]

One of the great films of our time was about the depression years, *Places in the Heart.* You may recall that last scene in the film. The congregation is taking Communion in a little, ugly country church. The people are singing: "This is my story, this is my song, Praising my Savior all the day long." As they sing, the little cups of grape juice are passed and a strange thing happens. Suddenly the whole movie cast is all there in that little church. Sally Field's dead husband sits beside her, young and strong. The young, drunk black man who had killed the husband and was later lynched sat on the pew beside them. Behind him were the Ku Kluxers who had done the lynching. On another pew there sat a couple who had broken their marriage vows and were hopelessly separated. Now they held hands and smiled. The whole sorry lot was there eating the bread and taking the cup. They made the connections and the walls that separated them fell down and the great unity for which Christ prayed long ago began to take place.

The sermons we preach are to make connections between the poor in body and spirit. Our words are to bring healing for the brokenhearted and deliverance for every sort of captivity. Our sermons are to give sight to the blind and liberty to the bruised. Our messages are to help whoever it is that comes find, in the chaos of their lives, the Lord's favor for them and all they love.

Next Sunday they will all be there as they were in Nazareth long ago-- the angry ones, the tired ones, the lusty ones, the young ones, the very old, the pious, and the burned out. You will stare out at the blind and the sick and the captives of a very secular culture. And if you have returned to the Source, what happened in Nazareth may just happen again. They shall drink and be filled. For they, and even the gospel-hardened preachers, will find a filling.

Notes

1. George Herbert, "The Wisdoms," *The Penguin Book of English Christian Verses*, Peter Levi, Ed. (New York: Viking Penguin, 1988), 104.

2. Rollo May, *The Courage to Create* (New York: Norton, 1975), 19-20.

3. James Lynch, *The Broken Heart* (New York: Basic Books, Inc., 1977), 108-109.

4. Emily Dickinson, *The Complete Poems of Emily Dickinson* (Boston: Little, Brown and Company, 1960), 433.

5. Wallace E. Fisher, *Preaching and Parish Renewal* (Nashville: Abingdon, 1966), 19.

6. Walter Brueggeman, *I Kings* (Atlanta: John Knox Press, 1982), 22-27.

7. T. S. Eliot, *The Complete Poems and Plays 1909-1950* (Harcourt, Brace and Company, 1958), 110.

8. *Ibid.*

9. Halford E. Luccock, *In the Minister's Workshop* (Nashville: Abingdon, MCMXLIV), 156.

7

"Upon the Profession of Your Faith..."
Baptism

Why water? Water cleanses. Water buries. Water
purifies. Water renews. Water quenches thirst. Water brings growth. Water washes away the dirt. Water offers us a chance to begin again. Water, then, is
a symbol of what God's graceful act in Christ Jesus
can do for us all.
—Roger Lovette

Go therefore and make disciples of all nations, bap-
tizing them in the name of the Father and of the Son
and of the Holy Spirit, teaching them to observe all
that I have commanded you; and lo, I am with you
always, to the close of the age (Matt. 28:19-20).

Do you remember your baptism? I remember some
things about that experience but not a great deal. I was
nine years old. I do recall it was a Sunday evening. My
baptism took place at the end of the worship hour. We
had one of those old-fashioned baptistries in the 1940s
that was located under the choir and the pulpit area. At
the end of the service, the choir would file down and sit in
the congregation. The organist and pianist would play
softly as the deacons removed the pulpit furniture. The
choir chairs would be pushed against the back wall. The
green velvet curtains that formed a modesty screen for
the choir would be pulled back. Then came the hard part.

118

The deacons removed section after section of the floor under the pulpit and the choir. Someone then darkened the lights. There was a single spotlight on the baptismal pool. I came out of a side door dressed in a white starched shirt and pants. The pastor was already in the water. I remember noticing that the water came up under his arms. He wore a black robe and extended a hand to help me down into the water. I recall shivering, even though the water was very warm. The only thing my pastor said to me was a whisper: "Are you afraid?" I shook my head that I was all right. It was then that he raised his hand and intoned those most solemn of words: "Upon the profession of your faith in the Lord Jesus and now in obedience to his commands, I baptize you, my brother in the name of the Father, Son, and Holy Ghost."

Let us put my experience down beside a service of baptism that dates back to A.D. 215. To begin with there was a careful examination of all who sought admission into the Christian fellowship. Idolaters, actors, circus performers and organizers, pimps, gladiators, harlots, astrologers, and magicians were rejected because of the immoral and pagan connotations attached to those life-styles. Soldiers and high government officials were not admitted because of their subservience to the pagan state. Artists and teachers were only grudgingly accepted. The church tried to draw a firm line between what she proclaimed and the pagan world on the outside.

Those who were admitted were called "hearers" and were required to enter a three-year period of instruction. They could attend the first part of the worship service— the Service of the Word—but were dismissed before the Lord's Supper. Only after a three- year period of careful instruction were the candidates admitted as "candidates" for baptism. A few weeks before Easter, each candidate was instructed in the gospel and carefully examined. On

Thursday before Easter, the candidates bathed. On Fri-
day and Saturday they fasted. On Saturday a final exorcism was performed by the bishop.

Saturday night was spent in prayer, reading, and instruction. On Easter morning, as the first light appeared,
a prayer was said over the baptismal waters. That prayer
spoke of the importance of water for the people of God.
They recalled the waters of creation, the water of the
grave, the crossing of the Red Sea, Moses and the water
from the rock. They remembered the water in Mary's
womb, the river Jordan and the living water the Christ
had spoken of.

The candidates were requested to remove all their
clothing and jewelry. The candidates were anointed with
two oils—the oil of thanksgiving and the oil of exorcism.
Then the candidates were led down into the water by a
presbyter or bishop.

In the water each candidate was asked, "Do you believe
in God, the Father Almighty?" After the candidate responded, "I believe," the presbyter would push the candidate down under the water. They were asked a second
question: "Do you believe in Jesus Christ, the Son of God,
who was born of the Holy Spirit from the virgin Mary,
and was crucified under Pontius Pilate, and was dead and
buried, and rose again the third day, and sat at the right
hand of the Father, and will come to judge the living and
the dead?" After the candidate nodded his assent he was
taken under the water a second time. The presbyter then
asked a third question: "Do you believe in the Holy Spirit,
the holy church, and the resurrection of the flesh?" After
the candidate said that he believed he was baptized a
third time.

Each baptized person was then anointed with the oil of
thanksgiving, clothed in a robe of white and led into the
congregation. After each candidate was confirmed by the
bishop, each convert knelt for the laying on of hands and

anointing. It was only then did the new believers become full members of the church. After partaking of the Lord's Supper for the first time they were reminded by the presbyter: "Once you were no people but now you are God's people" (1 Pet.2:10).[1]

It is no wonder that these new Christians remembered this experience all their lives. The Evangelical Church, with its strong emphasis on baptism as a regenerate experience must recover the importance and meaning of this command of our Lord. What are some of the things we might do to make this experience as meaningful to our new converts and the church as that experience was in the first century? This chapter will offer ways which I hope will help make baptism one of the most meaningful actions of the church.

Prepare the Candidates

No baptismal candidate should be baptized without careful instruction. We do not believe the baptismal waters have magical power. Baptism, in our tradition, is a symbol of what God has done in the life of the believers. No candidates should be baptized until they understand the meaning of baptism.

One matter that should not be left to chance are the practicalities of baptism. Children, especially, could benefit from such instruction. Never assume anything. Some are afraid of water. Others want to know what order will they come in. They will be concerned about where will they dress. Explain to each candidate where the pastor will stand and what will happen. Practice exactly what you will do and say. Explain carefully the words you will use and what they mean. Give them plenty of time for questions.

Take the new converts to the robing room ahead of time. Show them where they will dress. Take them to the baptismal pool and explain how deep the water is. Let them kneel down and touch the water. Prepare the candidates for baptism. Such acts may seem trivial but attention to the candidate's concerns may just make this a meaningful experience for those to be baptized.

Devote the Whole Service to Baptism

As you make the whole service the focal point, you are saying something powerful to your people: baptism is an important occasion in this church. We are just beginning to realize that the Lord's Supper loses much of its meaning when tacked on to the end of the worship hour. The same is true of baptism. Prayers, Scripture, music should all focus around the act of baptism. If baptism is a witness to the power of the resurrection, we should use all the resources at our disposal to make baptism more meaningful.

Use the service as a time to talk about the meaning of baptism. Through sermon or meditation redefine baptism. Many of those gathered still identify baptism with conversion. Little children and adults misunderstand this ordinance. Clarify your church's doctrine of baptism. Keep it short and make it so simple that even a child can understand.

A British Baptist prayer book expresses baptism's meaning in simple terms. 1) Baptism is an act of obedience to the command of our Lord Jesus Christ. We are baptized because He asks us to follow Him into the water. 2) Baptism is following the example of the Lord Jesus who was baptized in the river Jordan. We are baptized because our Lord was baptized. 3) Baptism is a public confession of our faith in Jesus Christ as Savior and Lord. We are baptized as a public testimony to our newfound faith. 4) Baptism is a vow or pledge of allegiance to the Lord Jesus that we will follow Him forever. Baptism, then is a promise that we make to God concerning our commitment.[2]

Let the Candidates Share Their Faith

Give some time for the baptismal candidates to share their testimony of faith during the service. You might call the candidates forward before the baptism actually takes place or ask them to express their faith as they stand in the water. Ask each new convert two questions:

> Pastor: Have you, (name), repented of your sins and asked God to forgive you and do you have faith in the Lord Jesus as your Savior?
> Candidate: I do.
> Pastor: Do you promise, as you depend on divine grace, to follow Jesus Christ and to serve Him forever in the fellowship of His church?
> Candidate: I do.[3]

Promisekeeping is at the heart of commitment to God. By asking each new convert to pledge their allegiance to the Lord Jesus and to the church you are underlining the importance of this occasion.

Let the Church Support These New Believers

After the candidates have pledged that they will follow Jesus Christ through His church, let the church family share in a response. You might ask the church:

If you, as a congregation, pledge your support to these new Christians, to pray for them and to accept them as your brothers and sisters in this fellowship, would you please stand to signify your love and care for these new members of our church.

Another way that some congregations have underlined their support of these new believers is through the laying on of hands. For years English Baptists have used this ancient rite to set aside believers. What better way for the church to show their love and care for these new Christians than to lovingly lay hands on each candidate as they kneel and whisper a prayer for each one of them? This old biblical rite gives each member of the congregation an opportunity to participate fully in the act of baptism. Someone might sing a hymn of commitment or the organist might play softly as the people slowly come forward for this ceremony.[4]

After the members have shared in the laying on of hands you might have a prayer of commitment for these new Christians. It is moving to have some parent, mate, Sunday School teacher, or church leader to offer the special commitment prayer at this time.

Make Baptism Personal

As each candidate stands in the water with the minister, the pastor has an excellent opportunity to make this baptismal experience personal. The minister might say: "Ruth, do you remember when we were meeting in our discipleship class? We said that water is used to wash us clean? As you stand here today I would have you remember that Jesus has washed you clean all over. As you are baptized remember that: 'If we confess our sins he is faithful and just, and will forgive us' "(1 John 1:9).

Plan to say something specific for each candidate about to be baptized. Another example is: "Tom, right now you are surrounded by the water of baptism. It is warm and feels good, doesn't it? This water is really a symbol of the love of God that surrounds you. Wherever you go, whatever you do, do not forget this day and the warmth of this water. The Bible is right when it says: 'Nothing can separate you from the love of God.' " (See Rom. 8:39.)

Another way to personalize this time in the service is to give each new Christian a special Scripture verse. The

Bible abounds in great challenges to the believer. The pastor might say something like: "Mary, since this is a special day in your life, I want to give you a gift this morning to take with you forever. This gift comes from the Word of God. This will be your special Bible verse as long as you live: "You are the light of the world . . . . Let your light so shine before men, that they may see your good works and give glory to your Father who is in heaven" (Matt. 5:14-16). You could use one of the Beatitudes as your gift to the candidate. You might use a verse from the Psalms: "The Lord is my shepherd, I shall not want" (Ps. 23:1). You might use one of Paul's beautiful challenges like: "My grace is sufficient for you, for my power is made perfect in weakness" (2 Cor. 12:9), or "Through God you are no longer a slave but a son, and if a son then an heir" (Gal. 4:7).

The key to giving each candidate a Scripture verse is to keep the verse simple and to make it some verse that they can carry with them throughout their lives.

After these personal words of Scripture gifts baptize these candidates.

Use Music Effectively

All the music in the baptismal service ought to reflect discipleship, commitment, salvation, and baptism. As the laying on of hands takes place you might have the choir sing softly: "Wherever He Leads I'll Go" or some other hymn of commitment. As the candidates leave the sanctuary to prepare for baptism you might have the congregation sing: "On Jordan's Stormy Banks," "I Have Decided to Follow Jesus," or another appropriate hymn.

One of the most meaningful responses the church can make is to sing immediately after each candidate is immersed. Suggestions will be made in the chapter on music, but have the congregation sing the Doxology, a chorus of "Blessed Assurance," or a separate verse of "Amazing

Grace" for each candidate or another appropriate congregational response.

After the candidates have dressed, bring them back into the service, and give them some personal symbols of their baptism experience.

Symbolize the Candidate's Baptismal Experience

Call each candidate forward and present them with some mementoes of this special occasion. A Bible with their name inscribed on the cover might be an appropriate gift. In the inside cover have the candidate's name, date of baptism, the church's name, and the pastor's signature. Baptismal certificates can be ordered for this occasion which are attractive and underline the importance of this moment in their lives. Some churches give small wooden cross necklaces that members can wear around their necks. Others give small aluminum crosses which can be carried in pockets or purses as a symbol of discipleship.[5] If you choose to give each new member a special Scripture verse, you might have someone write their verse in calligraphy and present it to them at this time.

Someone has said that there are two great moments in our lives—the day we are born into the world and that day when we come to understand why we were born. We mark that first event with birthday celebrations year after year. The second birthday is that holy occasion when we are baptized into the Christian fellowship. Let us, as Christians, make sure that this *why* of life is just as important in our life stories as the *when* of our lives. Plan on making baptism a significant occasion for new converts and it will be remembered all their lives.

Notes

1. William H. Willimon, *Word, Water, Wine and Bread* (Valley Forge: Judson Press, 1980), 30-33.

2. Ernest A. Payne and Stephen F. Winward, *Orders and Prayers for Church Worship* (London: The Carey Kingsgate Press, 1962), 132.

3. In 1742 The Philadelphia Association approved "singing the praises of God in Psalms, hymns, and spiritual songs," and "laying on of hands with prayers upon baptized believers." Note Payne and Winward, 132-133, for a structure for the laying on of hands at the time of baptism.

4. Payne and Winward, 136-138.

5. Small aluminum crosses can be ordered from Agora, P. O. Box 54342, Atlanta, Georgia 30308.M

8

This Do

Once in a group we were asked to name the warmest room in the house where we grew up. The leader wanted us to describe the room where we felt safest and most secure. The room, I think, that represented home. As we moved around that circle, it was amazing to hear the answers. Most everybody named the kitchen. We felt warmest in the place where we sat down and ate together. The church has gathered around a table for two thousand years and found a family and bread and a cup for the journey and a place of incredible warmth.

—Roger Lovette

And day by day, attending the temple together and breaking bread in their homes, they partook of food with glad and generous hearts, praising God and having favor with all the people (Acts 2:46-47).

Lyle Schaller, church consultant, has written that in the 1950s the common pattern in several mainline denominations was to offer the Lord's Supper once a quarter. But he says that practice is changing in many congregations today. All over the land churches are rediscovering the power of communion. Some congregations celebrate the Supper weekly, and a great many churches schedule the ordinance monthly. Schaller says that many of these churches have discovered worship attendance improves on those Sundays when the Lord's Supper is

scheduled.Other churches report that when they made
the change their worship attendance was down on those
Sundays when the Lord's Supper was observed.[1]

One of the reasons that attendance may drop on those
Sundays when the Lord's Supper is served may be poor
planning. Many church members do not have fond memories of the Lord's Supper. On those Sundays when they
enter the sanctuary and find a white cloth draped over
the communion table, many worshipers inwardly groan.
After the "regular" service is over, they sit down again
and the Lord's Supper service begins. It is no wonder that
many worshipers dread this occasion—they see the Supper as an appendage to worship—tacked on at the end
when their children are restless and they are hungry.
Such treatment speaks a powerful message to the people.

Our Lord said: "Do this." And if this important command is to be followed we must struggle with creative
ways to restore meaning and power to the Lord's table.
What are some of the things we can do to follow this command of our Lord in more than a perfunctory manner?

Devote the Whole Service to the Supper

Nothing proclaims this act is an important occasion
more than devoting the whole hour to the Lord's Supper.
If this is, indeed, a time when "we show forth the Lord's
death until he comes again," the Supper should be a high-
priority item for the church.

The Lord's Supper is an "acted out" parable. The action
of the meal speaks for itself. The bread broken and the
cup shared say something powerful about the gospel message. Christ Jesus was nailed to a cross, and His blood was
spilled for the likes of us. Little explanation need be giv-
en. Let the parable speak for itself.

All the components of the service can undergird the action of this central symbol. Plan carefully so that music,
prayers, sermon, and Scriptures all focus on the Supper.

The body broken and the blood shed for the forgiveness of our sins is a powerful evangelistic tool.

Remove the Communion Covering

You may remember the story of the young woman who decided to cook her first ham after she was married. She took the ham, cut off both ends, placed it in a pan, and then put it in the oven to bake. Her husband asked her why she had wasted so much of the ham. She told him that her mother had always cut off both the ends of the ham before she baked it and it was the best ham she had ever tasted. When they visited her parents, she asked her mother why she had cut off both ends of her ham. The mother said, "I don't rightly know, but my mother did it and she baked the best hams I have ever eaten." At Christmastime they asked the grandmother why she cut off both ends of the ham before she cooked it. She laughed and said, "Because my pan was too small."

This story might explain the presence of the Communion cloth in many churches. Why do churches cover the elements until the time of the Lord's Supper observance? This practice probably goes back to the early days in the church's life when sanitation was a problem. They covered the elements to keep the flies away. Since then, times have changed. Sanitation is no longer a problem, yet we keep lopping off both ends of the ham, never daring to ask where such a practice began. Why not do away with the cloth entirely? This custom served us well in former days. But that day has passed. Have your committee prepare the elements and leave the elements for all to see as the service progresses.

Several years ago many liturgical churches moved the communion table from the altar area and placed it on the level of the people. Such an act pointed toward a powerful truth. The Lord's table is spread for the people of God. By removing the covering, we say that the tokens of His broken body and spilled blood are ever present for all the people of God.

Preach on Communion

There is no better way to focus on the importance of the Supper than for the pastor to preach on communion. It might be a good idea to have a shorter message than usual if the whole service is to be devoted to the meal. But the preached word offers the pastor a great occasion to explain the importance of what the church is about to do. The Bible abounds with great themes that can make the Communion sermon meaningful.[2]

Vary the Ways You Take Communion

The way we receive Communion says a great deal about how God comes to His children. Sometimes we passively wait for the deacons to serve us the elements. This action speaks of God's initiative and how we partake of the graceful acts which we are given. The grace of God comes to us where we are and we benefit.

On some occasions we might change the structure completely and arrange for people to come to the table and receive the elements. This action by the people reflects those times when we take the initiative, we come with our needs, we reach out and take these things which God has provided. Something powerful is at work when we leave the safety of our pews and come forward to receive the good gifts which God holds out for us all. One variation on this is to have kneeling benches arranged so that people not only come, but can kneel to receive the bread and the cup.

One Sunday you might incorporate both principles of God's grace and our initiative. You might have the deacons to serve the bread to the congregation in the pews and then you might let the people come forward and receive the cup. A sermon could easily be preached on the twofold dimension of the Supper: God's grace and the people's initiative.

Any change in your order of service which might be unusual for your people should never be done without preparation. People do not like surprises. They want to know what is going to happen ahead of time. You might begin that preparation with the deacons, then other leadership in your church, note the changes in your newsletter, and even use part of the sermon time to explain what changes will be made and explain them in great detail.

Am I Invited?

A friend told me about a funny experience that happened in the church where he is a member. In the newsletter the church announced that the next Sunday they would have the Lord's Supper. One new Christian with little church background saw the notice in the church paper. She asked my friend, "This Supper thing. Am I invited and how much will it cost?" Part of the worship leader's task is to carefully explain that the Lord's table is prepared for His disciples.

One effective way to issue the invitation is to use the ancient invitation that we find in the *Book of Common Prayer:*

> Ye who do truly and earnest repent of your sins, and are in love and in charity with your neighbors, and intend to lead a new life, following the commandments of God, and walking from henceforth in His holy ways; draw near with reverence, faith, and thanksgiving, and take this Supper of the Lord to your comfort.[3]

One minister has said that a great variation on this wonderful summons is to change "Ye . . . who are in love and charity with your neighbors . . ." to read: "You *who want to be* in love and in charity with your neighbors".[4] Such a change draws the circle wider and allows those people whose relationships are broken to be brought into the circle.

For years our church has linked the invitation to another invitation:

> Come to this table, not because you must but because you may; come to testify not that you are righteous but that you sincerely love our Lord Jesus Christ and desire to be His true disciples. Come, not because you are strong, but because you are weak; not because you have any claim on heaven's rewards, but because of your frailty and sin you stand in constant need of heaven's mercy and help; come not to express an opinion, but to seek a Presence and to pray for a Spirit.[5]

Another variation on this same theme is to have the people say these words. They can be arranged so they make a strong invitation to the Supper.

> Leader: We come to this table,
> People: Not because we must but because we may;
> Leader: We come to testify not that we are righteous
> People: But that we sincerely love our Lord Jesus Christ and desire to be His true disciples.
> Leader: We come, not because we are strong,
> People: But because we are weak.
> Leader: Not because we have any claim on heaven's rewards,
> People: But because in our frailty and sin we stand in constant need of heaven's mercy and help;
> Leader: We come, not to express an opinion,
> People: But to seek a Presence and pray for a Spirit.

Another invitation that could be used by the pastor or used as a responsive invitation is:

> I come, not because I am worthy; not for any righteousness of mine; for I have grievously sinned and fallen short of what, by God's help I might have been.
>
> I come, not because there is any magic in partaking of the symbols of Christ's body and blood.
>
> I come, not from a sense of duty that is unacquainted with deep appreciation for this blessed means of grace—the highest privilege in Christian worship.
>
> I come, because Christ bids me come. It is His table, and He extends the invitation.
>
> I come because it is a memorial to Him, as often as it is done in remembrance of Him. Here is a vivid portrayal of the redeeming sacrifice of the Christ of Calvary. His matchless life, His victorious sufferings, and His faithfulness even unto death, are brought to mind, and I bow humbly before Him and worship.
>
> I come because in contemplation of the Father and His Son our Savior, I am moved to thanksgiving for so great a salvation.
>
> I come because in this encounter with the Savior I am made to feel the wrongness of my sins, base desires, unchristian motives, harmful attitudes, vain ambitions, and the things I have failed to do which God expected me to do. I acknowledge my utter unworthiness and walk again the painful, but necessary, path of repentance.
>
> I come because forgiveness comes with true repentance.
>
> I arise with the assurance of pardon, rejoicing in the opportunity of a new beginning.
>
> I come because I want to experience high communion with God the Father, revealed in Jesus Christ, and ever present in the Person of the Holy Spirit. And, having fellowship with Him, I am drawn closer

to all who kneel with me at the altar and, indeed, I become conscious of my kinship with all men everywhere who claim my Christ as Savior, the Holy universal fellowship of believers.

I come because I arise from the Lord's Table with new strength, courage, poise, and power to live for Him who died for me.[6]

Before the bread is broken and the cup served, the beautiful words of a great invitation say clearly who is invited.

How Much Will It Cost?

The woman asked my friend if she could come to the Supper, and she wanted to know what it would cost. The apostle Paul warned that we must not take the supper unworthily. This is not a casual meal. The broken bread and the cup that are shared reflect the heart of our faith. Paul challenged the Corinthians: "to examine themselves."

The Supper, then, is a great time for the church to confess all those things that make us less than God demands. Before the Supper, provide occasions for the people to confess their sins.

A time of silence is often an excellent way for the church family to begin to think of their lives and the things they need to confess.

On other occasions the worship leader might lead in a corporate confession. Psalm 51, already mentioned, could be a responsive reading where the whole church confesses their sins. Other Scriptures lend themselves to corporate response. The prodigal's repentance could be a great confession:

Father, I have sinned against heaven and before you; I am no longer worthy to be called your son (Luke 15:21).

This could be followed by the pardon of the father:

> But the father said, . . . "Bring quickly the best
> robe, and put it on him; and put a ring on his hand,
> and shoes on his feet, and bring the fatted calf and
> kill it, and let us eat and make merry; for this my son
> was dead, and is alive again; he was lost, and is
> found" (vv.22-24).

Another way to reckon with the costliness of the Supper is to have those gathered to write out their confessions before they take of the supper. They might write
them down and then keep them. One evening we had the
ushers to receive the confessions like an offering. Then
they brought the confessions to the table and we read
them one by one and after each confession, the people
said: "Lord, have mercy." The people were told that
evening to make their confessions anonymous enough
that no one would know who wrote them. After the confessions were read, Communion was served.

One of the most moving Communions we ever had was
on a Maundy Thursday evening. Over to one side there
was a large wooden cross with a spotlight on it. Most of
the lights in the sanctuary were off. We asked people to
come to the cross, leave their written confession pinned to
the cross, and then come to the table to receive Communion. No one present will ever doubt the costliness because of that Supper celebration.

Use Your People

Ordinarily, in most churches deacons serve the Lord's
Supper. This is a symbolic act since the word, *deacon*,
comes from the Greek word, *to serve*. This is appropriate.
You might expand the deacon's role in the Supper by asking them ahead of time to have the prayer for the bread
and the cup. Such prayers should not be haphazard but
should be planned to reflect the whole service. Other

ways that deacons or other members of the church might be used during the service are through responsive readings. You might let your deacons or another member lead in the time of confession.

The church need not restrict its prayer at Communion time to deacons and clergy only. Some Sunday ask other members of the congregation to come forward and to bless the bread or the cup.

During Youth Month one year our church was seeking greater ways that our young people could participate in the work of the church. With deacon and church approval, we asked the youth deacons to serve Communion during Youth Month. The deacons met with the young people and explained what they were to do. On the Sunday of the service, the youth deacons filed in and sat on the front rows. The elected deacons of the church sat behind them. Those young people that served Communion developed a new understanding of the role of deacons and the importance of communion.

The Role of Music in Communion

Probably nothing highlights the importance of the Lord's Supper in the church as does its music. Appropriate music can help make the difference in success or failure in this special time in the life of the church.

All the hymns for the day should focus on the Lord's Supper event. One great way of having the congregation participate in the Supper is to have them sing their confession just before the Supper is given. We have already suggested the use of the new hymn, "O Lord Jesus, Cast Our Sin Out, " but there are a multitude of hymns that can be used for this purpose. A prayerful singing of "Lord, I Want to Be a Christian" is another way to begin the people's preparation for the meal. You might have them sing, "Let Us Break Bread Together on Our Knees" or

have the choir sing Buryl Red's "In Remembrance of Me"
from *Celebrate Life.*

Another way to use the congregation through music is
to have them participate during the passing of the elements. As the congregation is served, have the people quietly sing, "They'll Know We Are Christians By Our
Love," "My Jesus, I Love Thee," "Nobody Knows the
Trouble I've Seen," "Amazing Grace," or "In Heavenly
Love Abiding." Sometimes you might vary this approach
and let the choir or some soloist sing during the passing of
the bread and the congregation sing during the passing of
the cup. The hymnal abounds in appropriate music for
such an occasion. You need not be tied to Communion
hymns. Use your imagination and you will see the variety
of musical offerings that can be used to make your Lord's
Supper occasions when your people "see the Lord."

The Special Times

The special occasions in the life of the church provide a
great opportunity for meaningful Lord's Supper
observances.

The early church made that first Communion for new
converts a time they would never forget. The converts
could not even be present for the Lord's Supper celebration until they were baptized. Those of us who ignore this
teachable moment for new converts are missing one of
the great educational opportunities for ministry. Invite
the candidates in early on the morning of their first
Lord's Supper celebration. Explain to them what the Supper means and why the church has held on to this tradition for 2,000 years. Explain the meaning of the bread
and the cup and confession and the whole service.

Invite the candidates to sit at the front or call them forward just before the Communion service begins. After all
are served, the pastor will go to each new convert and
hand them the elements. As they are served the pastor

might say: "This is your first Communion as a Christian. Remember that the body of our Lord was broken for you." When the cup is served, he might return to the new converts again and say: "Remember that this cup which I give you is a symbol of the shed blood of the Lord Jesus for the remission of your sins." Many churches give the new Christians the cup they have taken Communion from that day as a reminder of this special occasion.

Special seasons of the church year are great times to introduce change in your Communion service. People are more apt to accept something different at these times if they are prepared than they are on ordinary Sundays.

Thanksgiving is an appropriate time to take the Lord's Supper. The early church called the Supper the Eucharist, a thanksgiving for all that God had done in Jesus Christ. So the Thanksgiving season becomes a great time to focus on Communion. In the church where I serve, we have a special Thanksgiving Communion service on the evening before Thanksgiving Day. We meet in the fellowship hall around the supper tables. Each table has a Communion tray and a loaf of ordinary bread. The mood is more informal in the fellowship hall than it is in the sanctuary. We ask different laypeople to talk about the things they are grateful for. And then we ask any present to stand and tell of the things they are thankful for. After this time of sharing, we take the Supper. This has proven to be one of the most memorable times in our church's life together.

Plan a special Lord's Supper service during the Christmas season. Many churches are discovering Christmas Eve Communion is one of the favorite services for their people. Candlelight down the aisles, a darkened sanctuary, a Chrismon tree, the lighting of the Advent wreath, Christmas carols, poinsettias, and a candlelighting service all provide a great context for the Lord's table. For years our church has begun this service from the balcony.

The Choir would sing the call to worship from the balcony, a child would enter the sanctuary from the back with a lighted candle, march all the way down the aisle and light the Advent wreath. Some years we have used a child to begin the service by singing, as he or she moved down the aisle, "Come, O Come, Immanuel" or "Infant Holy, Infant Lowly." After the invocation have the choir and the ministers march in singing, "Angels We Have Heard on High." A descant on the last verse of that hymn fills the church with music and the people's hearts with joy. After the Supper is concluded arrange a candlelighting service and turn all the lights in the sanctuary off and let the people sing, "Joy to the World." Have the choir march out during this hymn with their candles still lighted. They could then sing the choral benediction from the back of the sanctuary. Such services make Christmas a memorable time for the people of God.

During Holy Week many churches have begun to observe the Lord's Supper on Maundy Thursday night. This was, historically, the night when Jesus first gave the Supper to His disciples. The word, *Maundy*, means mandate. It comes from the mandate that Jesus gave His disciples that night: "that you love one another as God loves you." As the Christmas service focuses on the birth of our Lord, this service underlines the importance of the cross and the death of Jesus. For years our church has used a chrismon tree for our Christmas worship. After Christmas, we take the tree, cut all the limbs from the tree, and construct a cross from the trunk of our chrismon tree. On the first Sunday of the Lenten season we arrange for our young people to bring that cross into the sanctuary as we sing something like: "When I Survey the Wondrous Cross." The cross is a stark reminder of the cross and the death of Jesus throughout the Lenten season leading up to Easter. On Maundy Thursday night we drape the cross in a purple cloth and a crown of thorns. This symbol provides a powerful centerpiece as we take the Supper.

On Easter some of our members come to the church early and decorate the cross with lilies and greenery. The stark cross becomes the cross triumphant.

Plan special Communion events during the life of your church year and you will find that people will come and find the hungers of their lives undergirded and blessed at the table of the Lord. As we break bread together the great Lord of the church will have mercy on our souls.

Notes

1. Lyle Schaller, *44 Ways to Increase Church Attendance* (Nashville: Abingdon Press, 1988), 75.
2. For an excellent sourcebook to help you think about the variety of ways that preaching might be used in Communion, you might find help in William H. Willimon's, *Sunday Dinner* (Nashville: The Upper Room, 1981).
3. Quoted in James L. Christensen's, *The Minister's Service Handbook* (Westwood, NJ: Fleming H. Revell Company, 1960), 30-31.
4. Robert A. Raines, *The Secular Congregation* (New York: Harper & Row, 1968), 99.
5. Christensen, 31.
6. Christensen, 31-32.

9

"When Bushes Burn"

God gives us just enough mountain peaks to make
it through the lonesome valleys.
　　　　　　　　　　　　　　　—Author Unknown

Now Moses was keeping the flock of his father-in-
law, Jethro, the priest of Midian; and he led his flock
to the west side of the wilderness and came to Horeb,
the mountain of God. And the angel of the Lord appeared to him in a flame of fire out of the midst of a
bush; and he looked, and lo, the bush was burning
and not consumed (Ex. 3:1-2).

Last summer I had the sad duty of cleaning out my
mother's house after her death. It was a journey down
memory lane. The hardest task I put off until last. I timid-
ly opened her cedar chest and began to sort through the
treasures of her life. She was a simple woman. She went
to work after finishing the 8th grade. She worked from
age 16 until 65 in a textile mill. The mementos of a lifetime were packed away in that cedar chest at the foot of
her bed. There was her 40-year pin for her years in the
mill. I found her children's birth certificates and tiny pictures of grandchildren. There was the yellowing clipping
of her father's death notice and a handful of Valentines
her children had given her years before. She had saved
old church bulletins and birthday cards. There was my
wife's 25-year-old engagement clipping. I discovered the
Bible the church had given her for being one of the oldest

members. There were pressed flowers and a lock of curly hair from a boy now turned man. And, of course, the gowns she never wore but saved for the hospital stay. There was a whole newspaper saved from the day FDR had died and crocheted pieces her mother had left her years before. It did not seem much for 82 years. And yet those tiny mementos marked the signposts of her journey. They told, in a cluttered kind of a way, of her own pilgrim's progress.

Life does not give us many mountaintop experiences. There are few days when we stand on the heights with a lump in our throats and see forever. But such moments come when we least expect them. God may give us just enough of these shining moments to trudge through our lonesome valleys. Packed away in our memories or in some small chest lie the treasures of our lives.

The people of God have always marked their signposts along the way. Like Moses, we all have days when the bushes of our lives burn brightly, when the purpose shines clearly before us. Isaiah knew it in the Temple. All his life was lived in the light of that wondrous moment when he saw the Lord high and lifted up.

So the Hebrews established special, holy days when they sang their songs on the way to Jerusalem. These were the times when their children were dedicated, circumcised, and brought into the larger family. They remembered a passing over, a death angel, and the providence of a good and loving Father. There were festival occasions for thanksgiving and prayers for the uncertain days that were yet to come.

Growing out of the synagogue, the New Testament church took those special days and made them their own. Baptism became a rite of passage. The Lord's Supper grew out of the Passover celebration. Christmas came to be that time when they remembered the Word made

flesh. Lent became that annual occasion when they prepared for Easter by meditating on the cross.

The Evangelical church has been suspicious of ceremony and special days. Yet the human spirit that hoards
away little snippets of life, craves those holy moments
when the bush burns and life is forever different. So the
task of worship is to provide modern pilgrims with signposts along the way. We, too, need times to remember, to
rekindle the fire, and to move on to the days ahead.

This chapter will offer suggestions that can enable the
worship leader and your people to discover the meaning
of their faith through the common events of life. We begin
with the special days of the church.

The Christian Year

The Christian year calendar came into being to enable
the church to see the vast panorama of the gospel story.
Through a rehearsal of that story week after week they
moved slowly from Bethlehem to Pentecost. Worship
leaders that construct their worship journey through the
Christian year give their people meaning and teach them
something of the continuity of the faith journey. First we
will look at the great Christian signposts that can give
our worship a biblical base year after year.

Advent.—The Christian year begins with the Advent
season. Advent is a preparation time. Through a retelling
of the old, old story, the church makes ready for the birth
of Jesus. Quite early the church learned that, without adequate preparation, the faithful would miss the deep
meanings of this holy season. Advent begins four weeks
before Christmas Day.

For several years we have begun our Christmas preparation with this prayer:

God, how we need an Advent. Some star to shine,
some voice to speak, some word, sandwiched in between

the news and the heartbreak, to burn its warmth into our cold hearts.

God, how we need an Advent. To help us remember what we have forgotten, to forgive us when we have sinned, to lift us when we have fallen.

God, how we need an Advent. To stand openmouthed and unashamed before the manger and wonder again at the miracle, the hope, and the possibility of it all.

God, how we need an Advent.

A beautiful centerpiece for this whole season is the Advent wreath. It is a circle that holds four candles. In the center is a larger candle. Each Sunday of the Advent season a candle is lighted until the circle is completed. After Christmas Day the large center candle is lighted.

During the Christmas season our worship service begins with the lighting of the Advent wreath. We use various members of our congregation to light the candles. Sometimes we use elderly couples, sometimes singles, sometimes families with small children. On some occasions we have used foreign students who were far from home at Christmastime.

After the prelude the designated members come forward. As they light the candles for the day, we usually have a reader, unseen, read the appropriate Scripture. As the Scripture ends, our choir sings: "O Come, O Come Emmanuel" or some other Advent hymn such as "Of the Father's Love Begotten." As the hymn ends we bow our heads for the invocation and our service begins.

Another variation on this lighting is to let those who light the candles also read the Scripture. A good way to explain the meaning of the Advent wreath is to print an explanation in the bulletin each week and to proceed with the candlelighting without announcement. Let the ceremony speak for itself. Our printed explanation reads like this:

On this first Sunday of Advent, we light the first Advent candle. There are five candles in the Advent wreath, symbolizing the four Sundays that lead us to Christmas Day. Each Sunday's new candle is lighted along with the previous candles until all four candles burn on the last Sunday before Christmas. The fifth candle is lighted on the Sunday morning following Christmas as a sign that the light has come in Christ Jesus.

After introducing your congregation to the Advent wreath you will find that your people will look forward to this occasion year after year.

Another service that is beginning to be popular in Evangelical circles is The Hanging of the Green. This is a festive occasion when the bare sanctuary is transformed slowly into a place of beauty during a service of worship. The Hanging of the Green is another step in our journey toward Bethlehem. Many congregations plan this ceremony for a Sunday evening. This is an excellent time to employ your children's choirs. In our church we use junior and senior high young people to bring in the garlands of green and the poinsettias. Senior highs bring in the characters of a large ceramic Nativity scene. As the infant Jesus is finally placed at the center the whole congregation is caught up in the reverie and wonder of this sacred season.[1]

Some churches are adding banners to their Christmas celebrations. Several years ago our young people made two huge 18-foot banners to hang on the walls of the sanctuary at Christmastime. One of these banners depicted the coming of the Wise Men while the other portrayed Joseph and Mary and the Christ child. Such projects take time and you must begin to work months in advance. But it is beautiful when young people will come into the sanctuary, years from now, and look up at Christmastime and tell someone: "I had a part in making that banner."

The chrismon tree is another valuable addition to
Christmas worship. The chrismon tree began in the Lu-
theran Church of the Ascension in Danville, Virginia,
years ago. That congregation was seeking for new ways to
make the Christmas season a religious event in the lives
of their people. They began to research the symbols of the
faith and then they began to make chrismons—mono-
grams of Christ and the Christian faith. These first ornaments were made of Styrofoam and were white and silver
and gold. The whole story of the Christian faith came to
light in those symbols. Then they brought in a huge tree
into the sanctuary, hung hundreds of white lights on the
tree, and placed the chrismon ornaments on the tree.[2]

Years ago our church adopted this practice. During the
season of Advent we have brought into the sanctuary an
18-foot tree. Members of our congregation worked all
year long making chrismons to decorate the tree. These
ornaments, along with the lights, were placed on the tree.
That chrismon tree was a beautiful addition to our
Christmas worship. Many Sundays during this season we
have gathered the children around the base of the tree
and talked about the meaning of the different symbols
that decorated the tree. Our candlelight Communion service on the eve of Christmas is a breathtaking sight as the
sanctuary is darkened and only the lights of the tree and
the flickering candles of the Advent wreath point our way
to Bethlehem.

Another suggestion that might make Christmas meaningful for your church is to bring back the old-fashioned
bathrobe drama and let the children take part in the nativity story. After reading Barbara Robinson's great
Christmas story, *The Best Christmas Pageant Ever*,[3] I began to see the possibilities of involving our children in the
greatest story ever told. You might use your children's
choirs at such a service. The nativity of our Lord comes

alive when the children of the church reenact the old, old
story of the birth of the Savior.

Instead of bemoaning the fact that the world has taken
Christ out of Christmas, the church can do many positive
things in worship to make this season moving and memorable for its congregation.

Lent.—As the Advent season prepares the church for
the birth of the Savior, the season of Lent prepares the
people of God for the wonder of Easter. For 40 days the
church struggles with the implications of the cross and
those times when Jesus "set his face to go to Jerusalem"
for the last time.

For years the liturgical church has begun the Lenten
journey on Ash Wednesday. This is the day of repentance
for the church. Several years ago we decided to try an Ash
Wednesday service. We had a simple service in our fellowship hall by candlelight after the fellowship meal. The
worship leader can set the stage by explaining that this is
the beginning of the Lenten season. On this night we begin to prepare ourselves for the resurrected Lord coming
into our lives again with power and grace. Ash Wednesday goes back to the Old Testament when the people of
God repented with sackcloth and ashes. So Ash Wednesday is a service of repentance and recommitment. After
an introduction, the pastor can invite the members of the
congregation to come forward and receive a sign of their
humanity and repentance. We used common soot as our
ashes. As the people filed by, the pastor will touch his fin-
ger in the ashes, mark the foreheads of those that come
and say: "Remember that dust thou art and to dust thou
shalt return." This service is a powerful reminder that we
are frail and weak and continually in need of the grace of
God.

On the first Sunday of Lent our service begins with our
young people bringing the cross into the sanctuary. As

the people stand to sing "At the Cross," or "When I Survey the Wondrous Cross," the young people slowly walk down the aisle and place the cross in an upright position in the front of the sanctuary. Some years the choir and ministers follow the young people into the church. We are reminded again of the power of the cross in our lives. That cross stands as a mute reminder during the seven Sundays of this holy season.

We have draped the cross in a purple cloth for Maundy Thursday service and on Easter some of our people come early and decorate that same cross with lilies and ivy as a symbol of the cross triumphant.

The Lenten season is a great time to focus on the passion narratives of the gospel. You might preach a series on the "Seven Last Words of Jesus" or the characters that we find around the cross. One of the most powerful services we had during that time was a service of nails. On that Sunday morning we gave each member a roofing nail as they entered the Church for worship. The service for the day began with a taped rendering of the hammering of the nails as a call to worship. During the silent prayer we played that tape again. I preached on "Nails" that morning. At the end of the service, after the benediction, the last thing the worshipers heard was the taped hammering of nails.

Many congregations have discovered new meaning during Holy Week with a special Tenebrae service. *Tenebrae* comes from the Latin word meaning *shadows* . During this service there are seven candles lighted. Through Scripture and song the congregation is led through:

The Shadow of Betrayal (Matt. 26:20-25)
The Shadow of Desertion (Matt. 26:30-35)
The Shadow on an Unshared Vigil (Luke 22:39-46)
The Shadow of Accusation (Mark 14:43-65)
The Shadow of Crucifixion (Matt. 27:27-38)

     The Shadow of Death (Luke 23:44-49)
     The Shadow of the Tomb (John 19:38-42)

After each Scripture passage is read, a hymn or choral piece is sung, a candle is extinguished until all seven candles are extinguished. The church is in total darkness. This darkness symbolizes the three days that Christ spent in the tomb. After a period of darkness and silence, the light returns. Sometimes this is followed by the Lord's Supper.

Maundy Thursday is the Thursday night before Easter. This goes back to that night in an upper room when Jesus met with His disciples for the Last Supper. The word, *Maundy*, comes from the Latin word, *mandate* . On that night Jesus gave His disciples a mandate that they love one another as God loved them. The service can easily be structured around these two great themes: 1) Love one another; 2) As I have loved you.

Years ago in Georgetown, Kentucky, our church used this theme for a Maundy Thursday service. The service was held in a large room. The Communion table was placed at the very center of the room and the elements were in place. Folding chairs were arranged on four sides around the table. But that night was different. The chairs were turned so they faced outward, not inward. As the worshipers sat down they could not see the table or the faces of others gathered. The worshipers stared at the backs and heads of those in front of them. As the worshipers sat down, they read these words in their printed program:

     You may find the arrangement of the chairs a strange one. Tonight they symbolize the separateness of the modern church. How many Sundays pass and we do not even know who sits across from us or sits next to us?

How much does this symbolize how little like a real fellowship we really are to one another?

The whole service was conducted in this manner until we came to the confession time before we took the Supper. We asked people to write the confession of their brokenness and place them in the offering plate which lay on the Communion table. Then they returned to their chairs and turned them around until they faced the table. When all the confessions were received and the chairs turned, people started coming to the table in twos and threes to receive Communion.

The shock of the chair arrangement was most effective. Moving to the table with their confession and then moving back to their places to turn their chairs around and then move back to the table to receive the elements made this a great experience for all gathered.[4]

Easter.—After seven weeks of meditating on the cross, Easter takes on new meaning. The stark cross of Lent gives way to the cross triumphant decorated with lilies and greenery.

A wonderful way to begin this service is from a microphone, unseen. The leader will say:

Minister: Do not be amazed; you seek Jesus of Nazareth, who was crucified.
People: He has risen, He is not here; see the place where they laid Him.
Leader: But go, tell his disciples and Peter that he is going before you to Galilee; there you will see him, as he told you (Mark 16:6).

After a triumphant call to worship and the invocation, have the choir march in as all sing: "Jesus Christ Is Risen Today."

Easter demands the best that we have: music, Scripture, sermons, and decoration. The church that struggles to make Easter a powerful testimony of the resurrection will help its worshipers understand something of the wonder and mystery those first eyewitnesses must have felt.

Pentecost.—After the Lenten season another great day for the church is Pentecost, 40 forty days after Easter. This day reminds us of the biblical promise when the disciples were to go to Jerusalem and wait for the coming of the Spirit. Pentecost is the birthday of the church. Without that mighty Wind that came to empower those grief-stricken disciples, there would be no church at all.

Use this occasion to talk of the work of the Spirit and the power of the Comforter in our lives. You might even have someone bake a birthday cake and use it, with lighted candles, during your children's time. If you work carefully this can be a teachable moment for all in the church.

The church that takes seriously the high days of the Christian year calendar can save its worshipers from falling into the secular trap. The old, old story becomes alive and powerful as we use the symbols of our faith.

While we must not fall into the secular trap, each congregation is wedded to two worlds. The world of faith and the world of everyday are always intertwined. Now we turn to some secular occasions that provide teachable moments for our people.

The Secular Calendar

Those who stumble into the house of God on any given Sunday bring many things with them. They bring their fears and their anger. They bring the joys and sorrows of their lives. We people of God are set down in a world of many concerns. The church that faces the world of today faces the challenge of touching people where they live.

Mother's Day and Father's Day.—These occasions provide an excellent time to focus on the family. Today's nuclear family is having a difficult time. Instead of focusing on another day when family meant only a father and a mother and two children, the church should expand its horizons and look at all those who gather. Such occasions as Mother's and Father's Days provide a time to talk about the family and its concerns. You might begin a family emphasis on Mother's Day and extend that until Father's Day. You might use this as a time to dedicate parents and children born during that year.

Several years ago we studied our Mother's Day service. Year after year it was bogged down with sameness and predictability. So that Sunday we asked for the women in our congregation to become our worship leaders. I will never forget a grandmother standing for her first time to deliver the invocation. Another mother read the Scripture, women served as ushers and led in the Scripture readings and the prayers for the day. Since that time people look forward to women leading our worship on this special day.

Fourth of July Sunday.—What better time to talk of the Christian's responsibility to the state than on July 4th Sunday? This is the time for singing national hymns, in recommitting ourselves to Christian citizenship.

On the 200th anniversary of our country we planned a service of worship as Baptists had worshiped 200 years ago. Men and women of the congregation that served as ushers were dressed in the costumes of 200 years ago. That service began with a man dressed in a period costume coming down the aisle with a Bible. When the Bible was in place, opened to the Scripture of the day, the service began. We lined the hymns that day as they did 200 years ago without books or instruments. Touching our past reminded us of our ties with our forebearers.

Beginning of the school year.—This is an important

time in the life of children and their parents. Those students going off to college or away from home for the first time face many decisions. This service provides the leaders in worship with a great occasion to deal with this momentous rite of passage for young people and their families.

One Sunday our worship program printed this meditation at the opening of the school year:

> Remember your first day at school? I was scared of everything. The kids, the strange new surroundings. Scared of having to sit down and mind when I had had six years of running loose and free. I was afraid of the teacher standing up there with her silver wire-rimmed spectacles telling us all the things we had to do. I was afraid of the Principal most of all. She was twenty feet tall, and had an office on the second floor. It was whispered the room was filled with all sorts of instruments of torture. The whole experience was strange and scary, and I did not know what to do. But I lived through it. I met a little boy who sat behind me who became my friend. My teacher held my hand when I was afraid and whispered that everything was going to be all right. I never did have to climb those long stairs to the Principal's office. I lived through it all. And in the riskiness of it all— doors opened, birds sang and windows opened to a larger world. Books and knowledge and new experiences were there for the asking. It begins with a risk: hard, life-threatening, scary, and full of promise.

One year we had a high-school principal read Arthur Gordon's beautiful story of the time he took his daughter to school for the first day.[5] Children of all ages identified with this rite of passage.

New Year's Day.—The new year is a great time to mark the passing of the old and the beginning of the new. This

is an excellent time to begin your Communion observance. As the elements were passed one year we had the
congregation sing:

> For all the blessings of the year,
> For all the friends we hold so dear,
> ....
> We thank thee, God.[6]

Through those simple words we lifted up the things of our
lives for confession and thanksgiving and benediction.

The new year provides us with a time for challenge.
The pastor may want to preach a sermon on "The State of
the Church" and map out the church's dreams for the
days ahead. This is an excellent time to observe the Lord's
Supper.

Besides the secular calendar, each denomination has
its own concerns that flow through the year of the church.
These, too, are teachable moments for the congregation.

The Denominational Calendar

The denominational calendar is important because it
ties the local congregation to a larger group of believers.
We are linked with a common purpose and understanding with other Christians around the world. The denominational calendar helps the local church expand its horizons and see the larger picture.

Missions.—Each church should provide the congregation with opportunities to see the importance of world
missions. Christmas is an excellent time to deal with foreign missions and to call for a special offering from the
people. A good way to deal with this would be to preach a
biographical sermon on one of the important mission figures in your denomination. Dr. Bill Leonard has given us
a model for this in one of his sermons.[7]

Some churches have a ceremony of flags and have

young people to enter the service with all the flags of the countries where the denomination has mission work.

The church that gives itself away to the world will be stronger and more world aware in its daily life and work.

Race relations.—The cause of race relations is still an unfinished business in our nation. The gaps between the races grows wider year after year. This occasion provides the congregation with a chance to see its responsibility to others.

One way that you might do this effectively is to have your minister of music plan a whole service of Black spirituals and sing the music that the Black Church has given us today. Then you might preach a sermon on the contribution of the Black worship and music to the life of the church today.

This is also a good time for exchanging pulpits with a black church or choirs. To sensitize our people to the challenge of race relations keeps faith with the last parable Jesus gave: " as you did it to one of the least of these my brethren, you did it to me"(Matt. 25:40).

World hunger.—The teachings of Jesus make clear that we who call ourselves Christians have some responsibility with the hurting of the world. World hunger provides us with a time to address that challenge.

Many churches use plastic rice bowls as a way to focus on world hunger.[8] These bowls could be given out earlier in the year. Members could be encouraged to place them on their kitchen tables and let the children have one for their rooms. Goals could be set for your hunger offering. On World Hunger Sunday, have the people come forward and present their rice bowls at the front of the church for world need.

One year I set up two tables at the front of the church and preached the sermon from those two tables. On one table I placed all the things a typical American family would eat in one meal. On the other table I placed the

items that a family in a ThirdWorld country would eat.
The contrast was striking. After presenting the need, you
might present the challenge of the Scriptures to address
this ongoing problem.

One Sunday as the ushers brought the gifts back to the
table, we sang together:

> Someone's hungry, Lord, come by here,
> Someone's hungry, Lord, come by here.[9]

During children's time one year I took a candy bar and
gave tiny bits of it to every child, and then I gave most of
the candy bar to one child and asked him to eat it in front
of the others. I asked him how good it was and to describe
how the chocolate tasted. Then I asked the other children
with their tiny bits of candy how they felt as one of their
friends ate most of the candy bar. We closed that children's time with a challenge to help the hungry.

World hunger will not go away in our lifetime, but the
church that points its people toward helping and loving
will go a long way in following the biblical admonition: "If
a brother or sister is ill-clad and in lack of daily food, and
one of you says to them, 'Go in peace, be warmed and
filled,' without giving them the things needed for the
body, what does it profit? So faith by itself, if it has no
works, is dead" (Jas. 2:15-17).

Turn to your denominational calendar and you will
find opportunities to help your congregation face a world
in need.

Local Occasions

There are special moments in the life of every congregation when the wick burns brightly and the people of
God rediscover purpose once more. These holy times provide the church with a chance to help its people worship
in meaningful ways.

Installation of a new minister.—What better way to introduce a new minister to the church than to plan a special service for that event? On this occasion, leaders of the community may be invited to come and speak a word of welcome. Some friend of the minister or the congregation could deliver a special challenge to the pastor and the church.

A moving way to install a new pastor is to have the pastor kneel at the front of the sanctuary and have the members of the congregation lay hands on him and set him apart for the service in that place. The church has called their new minister, why not now give them the opportunity to be involved in this old rite so heavy with meaning?

Installation of a new staff member.—This gives the congregation a chance to see the importance of other ministries besides the pastoral leadership. This becomes a great time to focus on the importance of Christian education, youth ministry, and other ministries of the church. Those staff members installed appreciate the fact that they are brought into the circle in a special ceremony that involves the whole church.

Ordination and installation of deacons.—Deacon ordination becomes a rich time for the congregation to see the importance of their lay leadership and their work.

You might devote a whole service to this event. Scriptures, prayers and sermon can all focus on service and the Deacon's responsibilities. A new hymn, written by Wayne Randolph, could set the stage for the service. This text can be sung to Haydn's tune, AUSTRIAN HYMN:

> For this rite of ordination
> We would come again to you,
> Asking that your holy presence
> Be with these what'er they do.
> Give them strength and dedication
> To withstand whate'er may come
> Let them know your wondrous power,

Let them spread it to everyone.

Give to them your love abounding,
So for others they might give
Love and peace your Son has died for,
Freedom for us all to live.
Be to them a strong assurance
As you were to Saints of old.
And whene'er the race is finished
Give reward to them untold.

As the hands are laid upon them,
Let them feel your presence here.
Be the source of all their wisdom
As they work both far and near.
As they minister to your people,
As they lead this Church for you.
Give them knowledge, lead them onward
As they stand for what is true. Amen.[10]

After the sermon you might call your new deacons forward and ask them, one by one:

_____ (name), do you believe that God has called you through this church to this special place of service?"
(Deacons respond yes.)
"Do you promise, as you depend on Christ for divine grace, to use your gifts here to the best of your ability for the upbuilding of the body of Christ?"
(Deacons respond yes.)[11]

This part of the service could be followed by asking those already ordained who are being set apart for another term to join the new deacons. You might ask them:

You have already been ordained by this congregation for service. But the church has asked you to serve again in

this important capacity. Do you covenant with this congregation to serve as a faithful deacon for the upbuilding of the people of God in this place?
(Deacons respond yes.)

Next, you might ask the people gathered:

If you covenant to stand by these new deacons and pray for the building up of the body of Christ here as they begin their new work, would you please stand?
(Congregation stands.)

After the people are seated, you might have the newly ordained deacons kneel at the front of the church. For years we have asked the ordained to come forward and to lay hands on these candidates. Why not ask the congregation that has chosen these deacons to all come forward and share in this ceremony. The church has selected these persons to serve; the church should set them apart. If your congregation is too large for all the people to come, you might have special persons designated to come along with some of their friends and family members to participate along with the ordained deacons and ministers.

As the people come forward someone might sing, "Lord, Make Me an Instrument of Thy Peace," or some appropriate selection. The organist might play quietly or the choir or congregation might sing.

Deacon ordination is a church act—a congregational activity. Enlarge the circle of responsibility. Let the people of God share in this great hour. Those set apart will never forget this special service in their lives.

Dedication of a new church building.—If there was ever a time for celebration it is in the completion of a building project. This becomes the time when the church family looks back on the history of the project, the early dreams, the meetings and the struggles, the financial campaign and the hard work of so many. All these should be lifted up in a great time of thanksgiving and praise to Almighty God.

At the First Baptist Church in Clemson, SC, we had worked for years on a project that included renovation of our sanctuary, adding a baptistry, enlarging our choir area, building a new educational building, and adding parking lots. We began that service with a remembering time:

Reader 1: It was in the early seventies and we were trying to decide what to do about facilities.

Reader 2: We formed a committee to renovate the old building but two properties came available and we scrapped the plans and bought the property.

People: *We come to remember . . .*

Reader 3: When we called a new pastor we asked him to help us with plans to renovate our building. So back to the drawing board we went. We had studies galore. Feasibility studies. Architectural studies. Engineering studies. We even employed an architect and began making plans.

People: *We come to remember . . .*

Reader 4: But interest rates were high; we had never built a building on our own; we grew afraid. Finally the project was scrapped.

People: *We come to remember . . .*

Reader 1: But in 1984 we went back to the drawing board. We employed another architect. We sought out fund raisers. Our Building Committee met for hundreds of hours.

People: *We come to remember . . .*

Reader 2: We wanted a larger fellowship hall, a baptistry where all could participate in baptism, we wanted to renovate our existing space, we needed a new choir suite, and offices to meet the needs of a growing church.

It seemed like we needed everything. Access to our buildings, more space for Sunday School and a building to meet a growing community. We needed more parking and more restrooms.

People: *We come to remember . . .*

Reader 3: Remember how scared we were when the figures were put on paper? Remember how hard we worked with our fund-raising? Remember that shining night at the Holiday Inn when so many had worked so hard? We pledged $950,000 before the month was over.

People: *We come to remember . . .*

Reader 4: So on faith we broke ground on May 31, 1987. Houses were moved, holes dug, asbestos was removed, rooms were gutted. We were on the way.

People: *So we have come to remember that we are a people of faith. That our prayers and hard work have come true. That God in His goodness has poured out His life on our efforts. That we have been stretched, one and all, for the kingdom of God. And, in remembering, we celebrate our victories!*

There were few dry eyes in the house that morning. We had come to remember and in the remembering something moved across that congregation.

These are the times when the bushes burn. The special moments when we take off our shoes for the place on which we stand is holy. It is a time for seeing the Lord, high and lifted up. Such moments are rare—but they provide the church with a purpose for the days ahead.

Notes

1. James L. Christensen, *New Ways to Worship* (Old Tappan, New Jersey: Fleming H. Revell Company, 1973), 75-80.
2. Information for making chrismons may be ordered from many local book stores.
3. Barbara Robinson, *The Best Christmas Pageant Ever* (New York: Avon Books, 1972)
4. This special Communion service by the author has been detailed in David Randolph's *God's Party,* (Nashville: Abingdon Press, 1975), 30.
5. Arthur Gordon, *A Touch of Wonder* (New York: Fleming H. Revell Co.1974).
6. See *Baptist Hymnal,* Walter Hines Sims, ed. (Nashville: Convention Press, 1956), 495.
7. Bill Leonard, *Word of God Across the Ages* (Nashville: Broadman Press, 1981), 77-87.
8. Rice bowls may be found in your local book story. If not, they may be ordered from Rice Bowls, Inc., Post Office Box 3216, Spartanburg, SC 29304.
9. Folk song.
10. "Hymn for Ordination" written by Wayne H. Randolph, Minister of Music, Second Baptist Church, Memphis, TN. Used by permission.
11. This idea came from: Ernest A. Payne and Stephen F. Winward, *Orders and Prayers for Church Worship* (London: The Carey Kingsgate Press, 1962), 211-217.

10

To Everything There Is a Season

Waiting for a dinner call one evening, I watched a weaver in Berea, Kentucky, weaving a piece of cloth. Her work was tedious and slow. The shuttle moved back and forth. She chose one thread and then another. It all seemed so monotonous. Slow. It took a long time. After dinner I returned to find the weaver still working. In that short hour and a half the pattern in the cloth was beginning to form. It was far from finished. But I could begin to see a design faintly emerge. Life is like that. The threads of our lives are woven, one by one, the small and the inconsequential, until, at some point, a pattern forms and life has a special shape.

—Roger Lovette

For everything there is a season, and a time for every matter under heaven. A time to be born, and a time to die; a time to plant, and a time to pluck up what is planted; a time to kill, and a time to heal; a time to break down, and a time to build up; a time to weep, and a time to laugh; a time to mourn, and a time to dance (Eccl. 3:1-4).

In Vivaldi's great musical masterpiece, *The Four Seasons*, the music is beautiful. As one first listens to the orchestra all the music sounds the same—full and strong, like life itself. But as one listens closely to the music one begins to hear the different sounds of the seasons. Vivaldi begins with the triumphant sounds of spring when all is fresh and clear. Soon, the sounds of spring give way to summer and the music takes on a deeper resonance. Then autumn comes with a deeper sound. Vivaldi ends on a muted note of winter. The music is still beautiful and full—but the sounds are different—one can almost feel the cold and the frost as the music ends.

Life, too, has its seasons. The day when we stood at some altar and said our vows. The special times when we made some commitment or dedicated a child. Holy moments when we felt the warmth of the baptismal waters or took the bread and the cup that first time. These were the days when our children were little, anniversaries, birthdays, driver' licenses, and first jobs. These were the New Year's Eves and confession times, Christmases and somber times when we said good-bye to some loved one for the last time.

The church that is wise will incorporate these hinge-turning moments into its life and work. People hunger for some ways that can fuse the meanings of their lives with the message of the gospel. So the rites of passage are part of the lives of the people of God. These rites must be marked if people are to live their lives in the context of a living faith.

Elton Trueblood has touched our pulse in *The Common Ventures of Life.* He wrote that the danger of our time is that the church touches the life of ordinary men and women at few meaningful points. Religion for most of them means churchgoing. Few find help or hope in their daily round of work, sleeping, governing, and playing and having children and suffering. Only as we fuse life with worship can we possibly help people find deep meaning in the things that make up their lives.[1]

Our culture is pervaded by secularism which, by its very nature, strips life from its religious foundation leaving people to seek other ways to find meaning in their lives. Trueblood said we have turned healing over to the

physician, death over to the mortician, education over to
the school, and work over to the labor union.[2] Faith,
pushed further and further from the center of life, becomes an abstraction. Life becomes flat and tasteless
without an eternal base.

Once upon a time the church spoke to the people from
womb to tomb. The church provided meaning for birth
and living and death. Worship provides those of us at the
end of the twentieth century with multitudinous occasions where we can help people, once again, see the Lord
in the common events of their lives.

This chapter will deal with two events that provide the
church with an opportunity to help people in the passages
of their lives. Other chapters have dealt with baptism,
with the special moments when the bushes burn. This
chapter will deal with marriage and death as teachable
moments in the seasons of life. To ignore these two important moments in the lives of the faithful is to send them
on their way bereft of the help they need for the days
ahead.

Marriage

The crisis of secularism can be seen in no place quite as
clearly as in the mounting divorce rate. Thousands of couples stand at some church's altar every year and yet
many of these marriages end in failure and
disappointment.

David Mace has said that each couple has a great ambi-
tion of creating a beautiful garden of their own. They
want it to be a place of peace and serenity with tall trees
and beautiful shrubs and flowers. We tell the couple that
we will help them. We give them a piece of vacant land
and the title deed. But we give them little else. Left on
their own the young couple is likely to purchase two lawn
chairs and settle on their land and expect the garden to
flourish. Nothing happens. Mace says unless they learn

something about soil chemistry, suitable plants, and something of arranging and planting, their dreams will not come true. They have to develop new skills and devote time and hard work or there will be no garden at all.[3]

When a young couple come to the church to be married, the church faces a tremendous challenge of helping them make their garden all they intended. The church is charged with helping the young couple see that a wedding is not a marriage. The wedding ceremony is only the prelude of a long and arduous process if their garden is to flourish.

What are some of the things the church might do to help the young couple and their families in the hard days ahead?

Make the wedding ceremony a Christian occasion.—For too long we have left the wedding to bridal consultants, the tastes of brides, and their mothers. The family gets so caught up in the logistics and the details that the larger issue of the wedding as a religious occasion is lost. It is time for the church to sound the note that marriage is an act of worship. We believe this is a holy moment when a couple stands at God's altar and pledge promises "for better or for worse" to one another. Each wedding provides a teachable moment where promise keeping is seen as part of our Christian commitment.

We open the sacred Book. We read Scriptures. We sing hymns and say prayers. We ask God's blessings on the couple, their parents, and all gathered. Music should reflect this setting. The church should put some parameters so that the music used reflects a Christian orientation.

When a young couple begins to understand that what happens at the altar is one of the most important occasions in their lives they will approach this time of promise keeping with greater seriousness. They will also appreciate a church that takes them and their commitment seriously.

Make the ceremony personal.—Each service has a predictability about it, and yet each couple is different. When they stand at the altar each man and woman brings something entirely different to the old words of "for better or for worse." So this becomes a time when the church interprets to the couple by the way they meet and plan that the church believes this is an important occasion and they are special. Listen to the requests of the couple and the families. Work patiently with them on details and arrangements. Incorporate the personalities of the couple into the service. A church that takes its people seriously will reap dividends in the years that follow.

One of the most moving wedding services I have participated in was that of a young couple who had both been divorced. They both had little children. After great pain, both of them had been through the trauma of divorce. After several years they met at a singles' retreat at a denominational meeting and finally decided to get married. They wanted a Christian wedding and they wanted a Christian home.

One afternoon a small cluster of family and friends met in the sanctuary. The bride came in a side door with her two children, the groom came in the other side door with his son. As they moved toward the center where they would be married, a friend played, "Jesus Loves Me" on the organ. They stood at the altar, along with their children. I asked those gathered to leave their seats and to surround the couple as a sign that they would support them and pray for them in the days ahead. Their families came forward, and friends who had been in singles' meetings with them. They had asked me to talk about promise keeping. They wanted me to explain to all gathered that they stood there after they had failed to keep the promises in another time and another place. They asked me to talk about the pain of separation and divorce. They wanted me to ask them publicly if they had asked God for forgiveness and sought as best they could to begin again. Then I talked about how the gospel provides us all with a chance to begin again. Prayers were offered that this union would last and God would bless their new beginning. Those gathered knew that they were participating in a high and holy moment.

Interpret the words to the couple and those gathered.— During premarital counseling, the pastor should use part of his time with the couple to explain the meaning behind the words. Each part of the ceremony becomes an appropriate outline to deal with this new adventure in promise keeping.

This same approach can be adapted at the rehearsal to teach all that are part of this occasion of the importance of the Christian wedding.

You could begin by welcoming those gathered. After a prayer for the couple and the friends you might break down the whole ceremony for all to understand what will take place.

1. Why are we here? We are here to join this couple in holy matrimony. Because this is a sacred occasion we ask God's blessing on what we are about to do. We read Scripture that sets in context the whole of marriage and this union. Sometimes we use a hymn or a solo to underline this whole concept.

2. The couple states their intention, "Do you take, _____ , to be your wedded husband?" This is the time when the couple says that they really are serious about this business of marriage. They state their intention to become husband and wife.

3. Next, the pastor gives a charge to the couple stating that this is a sacred occasion and that they are to keep the vows they are about to make.

4. After the charge, the parents are asked if they support this union. The old ceremony has the father to speak for both families when the pstor asks, "Who gives this woman to be married to this man." Such a question is really archaic. We own no one and we give no one away. It would be better if you would say something like: "Since the Book of Genesis God intended man for woman and woman for man. The biblical admonition was to: 'leave father and mother and to cleave to one another.' Marriage is having a difficult time today and this couple will need all the loving support of their family and friends if this union is to be strong. _____ 's father stands beside her. (Many times the groom's father is the best man.) _____ 's father stands beside him. They stand here as a symbol of the fact that they will support their children in this new union. I am going to ask the mothers to stand now as a symbol that they, too, will support, along with their husbands, this marriage of their children." (Mothers stand.) After this the mothers sit down, the father of the bride turns to sit with his wife, and the ceremony resumes.

You might then ask those gathered to pledge that they will support this couple by their prayers and love in the days ahead. They could do this either by standing or by saying: "We do."

By enlarging the circle to include the parents and all gathered we are saying that marriage is not an isolated act. This is a family affair. We need each other if our relationships are to be strong. Such a covenant to help and support are at the heart of the Christian understanding of faith.

5. Interpret to all those gathered the heart of the ceremony: promise keeping. The vows spoken are at the center of the service. This is what makes this whole occasion a Christian union. Have the couple to turn toward each other, hold hands, and speak their vows after the pastor.

6. Explain the importance of the ring ceremony. Rings are worn as a symbol of this new marriage. They pledge that they will wear them as a symbol of this new relationship.

7. The pronouncement and the final prayer come at this time. Here the couple is officially pronounced husband and wife and we bow our heads to ask God's blessing on them for the days ahead. A time of silence is often meaningful when all those gathered lift up this new couple to the care and keeping of the Heavenly Father.

In *The Spectator Bird*, Wallace Stegner tells the story of the old couple who have been married for many years. He likens that relationship to two old birds who have been through everything together.

> It is something—it can be everything—to have found a fellow bird with whom you can sit among the rafters while the drinking and boasting and reciting and fighting go on below; a fellow bird whom you can look after and find bugs and seeds for; one who will patch your bruises and strengthen your ruffled feathers and mourn over your hurts when you accidentally fly into something you can't handle.[4]

The church that takes time and trouble to help couples as they come to this important occasion strengthen the Christian understanding of marriage for all in the church.

Death

As the church cannot abdicate its responsibility at the time of marriage, we cannot leave the matter of death to chance. Ecclesiastes says there is a "time to die." Jesus said, in that first sermon, that one of the things He came to do was to "heal the brokenhearted." The church that takes seriously its ministry in the time of death will help its people understand the power of the Christian faith at one of the most difficult times in their lives. The funeral service helps family members and friends mourn in a genuine and healthy way.

The funeral service is a time for worship.—Like weddings, the church has often left the funeral service to local customs, the family, or the morticians. What results is often a sad occasion time that is stripped bare of faith meaning for those gathered.

The funeral service can be a time of worship for the people of God. What better place to have the funeral than in church? Many communities settle for the convenience of a funeral home. But what ties do people have to a funeral chapel? There is something deeply moving about having a funeral or memorial service in the place where one worships weekly, where your children were baptized, where you broke the bread and drank from the cup, and where your children were married. Sense of place is most important in our lives. Have the funeral service in a familiar place that ties the terrible experience of death to a sacred spot.

At that service it seems most appropriate to let those gathered participate in the service. Hymns of the faith can be sung, appropriate Scriptures read, prayers can be said for the family and all that mourn. The brief address can be part of that worship service.

One of the most moving services I have ever participated in was for a man who had only been a member of our congregation for a year before he died. He and his wife had moved to our town to retire. The man developed cancer and died less than a year later. But during that year he and his wife had joined a Sunday School class, had been involved in the lives of a few people. There were only a handful of people that knew this man. But we came into the sanctuary and everyone sat down front. I stood down front on the level with the people. After some Scripture and a hymn, I told them I was going to do something a little different. I was going to let them share with the family some of the things they remembered about our friend that had died. I had asked several people ahead of time to say a few words in case no one spoke spontaneously. Every person that spoke that afternoon was from the man's Sunday School class. There was a young lady that stood and talked about how he had been a grandfather figure to her little girl. Her own father was dead, and she would take her daughter to see him and she loved him. His Sunday School teacher spoke about the courage he had seen this man exemplify during his bout with cancer. Someone else stood and spoke of how they would be praying for his wife and the children. Six people spoke that afternoon and each one undergirded that family in a moving way. We left that service and moved to the fellowship hall where some members served refreshments. The widow had displayed their wedding album, family photographs, and pictures that were important in their life together. All those gathered knew they were part of the beloved community.

Make the funeral service a time for facing reality.—The Christian faith speaks realistically about death. Our whole culture is afraid of death. We deny death in almost every part of our society. But in church we are given a great opportunity to speak to the human condition.

Let the funeral service reflect reality. We express our sorrow. We talk about how hard it is to give our loved ones up. We tell family members we know how hard it is to lose someone after all these years. We talk about the guilt we sometimes feel and how long is the journey of grief.

But we affirm that we are not alone. The Father is with us. We talk about the promises of our faith and our belief in the resurrection. We keep our words short and direct. But we face the fact of our sorrow and we turn ourselves toward Him who came to heal all the hearts that were ever broken.

Make the funeral service a time for affirmation.— Hymns, Scriptures, remarks can all be directed toward the Christian belief in the resurrection. The people of faith do not despair. They do not deny their feelings, they face them head-on. But they know that they are not alone. Their loved ones are in the care and keeping of a loving Heavenly Father and those that are left have the promised Comforter to undergird and sustain them through all their lives.

Plan the same type of service for all.—One of the greatest compliments that I heard about a pastor friend came after a funeral service. The man who died was a quiet man whose circle of influence was not felt outside his own family. His widow said: "The Pastor made me feel that my husband was somebody." The task of the Christian faith is to make all feel like they are somebody.

One of the ways that we accomplish this in church is to plan the same type of service for all. Why should the greats of the world, the people of money or influence have some special service while the quiet people have an entirely different service? We say that at the foot of the cross the ground is level. The funeral service should reflect this theme. Prayers may vary, hymns may change— remarks for one service may not be appropriate for another. But in the Christian church all should be treated with the same respect and caring. The church that seeks ways to do this will find a greater authenticity in its message.

Some churches do this with the use of a funeral pall. The casket is covered so that no one knows one casket from another. This is a great leveler. Another practice many churches use is in not allowing a great display of flowers in the church service. Only one or two arrangements from the family are allowed. The rest remain in the vestibule or at the grave. God has no favorites. The church works hard to express this great truth.

Paul admonishes us to grieve but not as those who have no hope. The Church has the great opportunity to help its members grieve and know they are not alone. The Father and the community of the faithful stand with them. Such moments provide powerful undergirding for the fragile times in our lives.

The church that takes seriously the rites of passage in the lives of its people will never go out of business. It will lift up the seasons of life for benediction and blessing. And the people will go away strengthened, enriched, and challenged for the living of their days.

Notes

1. Elton Trueblood, *The Common Ventures of Life* (New York: Harper & Row, 1949), 20-21.

2. *Ibid.*, 21.

3. David and Vera Mace, *How to Have a Happy Marriage* (Nashville: Abingdon, 1977), 40.

4. Wallace Stegner, *The Spectator Bird* (New York: Doubleday, 1976), 213.

11

Hope for Years to Come

O God, our help in ages past,
Our hope for years to come,
Our shelter from the stormy blast,
And our eternal home!
—Isaac Watts

For I know the plans I have for you, says the Lord,
plans for welfare and not for evil, to give you a future
and a hope (Jer. 29:11).

On our better days the people of faith have been a forward-looking people. We have known that God was not finished with us—that there was still much for us to do.

As the 20th century slowly winds down, and we look forward to a new century, the challenge for the church is to provide worship forms that can enable us to face whatever comes with faith and purpose. This last chapter will offer suggestions that might help you and your congregation as you plan for the future in worship.

Breaking the Passivity Trap

Kierkegaard left us some solid advice for breaking out of the passivity trap. Most churches, he said, worship as if they believe the pastor is the actor, God is the prompter, and the worshipers are the audience. Such an understanding of worship leaves little responsibility to the people. The burden is on the minister to pull the whole thing

176

off. So they sit as observers, daring the worship leader to lead them in worship. Little change occurs in such a setting. Kierkegaard said that we must reverse the process. In the worshiping church, the pastor is the prompter, the worshipers are the players and God is the audience.

The great danger for today's church is to fall into the entertainment trap—to come as passive spectators while we merely observe the action someone else produces. Little change occurs when there is minimal involvement by the people.

Isaiah saw the Lord because he was the audience. The prophet was caught up in the wonder and mystery of the hour. He heard a voice. He was addressed, and consequently, was forced to make a decision which affected the rest of his life. Isaiah did not sit on the sidelines. He was an active participant in the life-changing drama of the ages.

So the church today must seek ways to move from spectator to participant. Involvement is the key to meaningful and life-changing worship.

Robert Webber has reminded us that worship is a verb.[1] This action is what *we do*. He says that worship becomes something we are drawn into when: 1) We prepare to worship; 2) we hear God speak; 3) we respond to God; 4) God sends us forth.[2]

What are some of the things we can do to enable our people to participate in the drama and break out of the spectator mold?

Recover the doctrine of the priesthood of the believers.— For years the pastor has dominated most worship services. In most churches the minister and other paid staff members do everything that is done in worship. They plan the service. When worship begins, they make the announcements, lead the prayers, preach the sermons, and give the benedictions. If it were not for the ushers, the choir, and the musicians, the worshipers would not even need to be present. Such attitudes resemble the old Roman worship where Mass was said whether worshipers were present or not.

One way to help your people is to involve many of them in worship opportunities. Call on your people to lead in prayers, to read the Scriptures, to make the announcements, to lead in children's worship. Church members that have not been used to being worship leaders will be wary of such responsibilities. But with a little training, your people can assume many of the roles that we have left to the clergy. Slowly, members of the congregation will begin to welcome these occasions and they will find worship taking on a new power in their lives. They will bring to their tasks the things of their lives and worship will breathe with the stuff of real life. Young people and adults of all ages can be brought into the circle of worship leadership. If liturgy is the people's work, it is time that we begin to let them do some of the hard work of helping our congregations see the Lord.

Form a worship committee.—Why should the ministers be the only persons in the church who work on worship preparation? Many congregations have discovered new life in calling forth interested laypersons to plan the services of the church. Through instruction and participation the services will have a new power.

This whole book has been an attempt to break out of the passivity trap. You will find here many ideas that may help you help your people worship by participation. It is my hope that the ideas found in each chapter will be springboards to use your own creativity to help your people discover how they may employ their gifts as worship leaders in your congregation.

Break Out of the Verbal Trap

The average church service is much too wordy. We have employed words to carry almost all of our work in worship. Most all our prayers are spoken. Most all of our responses are read. Most sermons are words, words, words. One would think that the verbal is the only approach to reality that we have today.

But we know from our own experiences that reality is multilayered. Real life is not abstract but concrete. And the difficulty with faith is trying to express the abstractions of faith in concrete and meaningful ways.

In marriage we use candles, flowers, wedding rings, and music to express the covenant relationship. When children are born we give balloons and gifts of blue and pink. We take pictures and send out announcements. We mark these moments in church with roses and special announcements. Anniversaries are celebrated with flowers and gifts. When death comes we take food by the house, send sympathy cards, memorial gifts, flowers, and come in silence to support our friends that grieve. Words are simply not enough to express the high and holy moments in our lives.

When it comes to matters of faith we must rely on words. Words, properly employed, do express our feelings on many occasions. Words like the Gettysburg Address help us see the kind of people we are to be. John Kennedy's, "Ask not what your country can do for you; ask what you can do for your country," call us back to our purposes as a nation. Martin Luther King's, "I have a dream . . ." speech stirs us to new visions.

Words in church can be used meaningfully to express matters of faith. They must be carefully chosen, simple, and easy to understand. Yet, like other areas of life, we cannot expect words to carry all the weight of our faith understanding.

Worshipers come into the service with many layers of reality. They bring the terrors of their lives which they do not understand. Sunday after Sunday they bring their griefs long unresolved. They come with fears, joy, confusion, and unconfessed sins, hoping that something will happen that will strengthen their lives and add underpinning to their faith journey.

David Randolph has suggested some of the layers of reality that go beyond the verbal in church.

1. The unconscious expresses itself through posture, gesture, movement, touch and other nonverbal ways.

2. Sound is one way of understanding reality.

3. The written word is an extension of speech and yet different from oral communication.

4. Sight communicates. We learn through what we see.

5. Images stir our lives. Stories of the boy that left and the son that stayed home speak to our lives. Words like *Father, Mother* bring back other times and places. Home and family take us way back to another place. We link our lives to the images that we fix upon.

6. Emotions touch us all. Anger, joy, laughter, grief should all find some logical expression in worship.

7. The social world around us is a way of perceiving reality. The people that sit around us—friends and strangers—are part of our reality.

8. Things communicate. Flowers, stained glass, offering plates, silence and hymns stir our imaginations.[3]

Discover ways to break out of the verbal trap in your worship. Bring all the levels of understanding into the church and your worship will breathe with the stuff of everyday life.

Training the Troops

Worship renewal is hard work. The worship leader that decides to make worship more meaningful will discover resistance, apathy as well as enthusiasm.

The worship leader must recover the teaching role as leader. The people's visions will never be broadened unless they are trained in how we learn and change and what biblical worship is all about.

A nation trained by television to be spectators needs much help and encouragement if they are to recover for themselves the doctrine of the priesthood of all believers.

You might spend sermon time, seminars, Sunday or Wednesday nights, or retreats as occasions to help your people come to terms with mystery and awe.

Lyle Schaller has said that good goals are those that we have a part in formulating. Bad goals are those that someone else has developed and want us to implement.[4]

Seek creative ways to train your people and this will pay dividends in the days ahead.

Making Free Worship Free

The principle that early Evangelical church leaders employed was a desire to unshackle the church from the cluttered forms that inhibited the spirit.

The people of God need to discover this revolutionary idea—that we are a free people under God. We have a right to seek new and creative ways that can make worship come alive for our lives and time.

The church must turn to the cutting edge of understanding the many layers of reality. Through studies of how we learn, we begin to appropriate alternative ways that can free the church to let the Spirit freely flow through the structures of our worship.

Why knows what the Spirit of God may have in store

for His people in this new day? New wine demands new wineskins. Those leaders and churches that are open to change and to the Spirit will be those churches that revitalize their people for such a time as this.

Drawing the Line

Our age has been called the "Me or My Decade." We have been accused of turning inward and being interested only in those things that concern us and ours. Much of what happens in church today reflects the narcissism of our age. The larger picture of a Christian in touch with his time, responding to the needs of the world Christ loved, gets easily lost in the shuffle of church growth and strengthening sagging budgets.

Worship must draw the line hard and fast between secular and sacred. The church that blurs that line is in danger of losing its identity and providing its worshipers with little of substance.

Dr. Robert Bridges says: "If we consider and ask ourselves what sort of music we should wish to hear on entering a church, we should surely, in describing the ideas, say, first of all that it must be something different from what is heard elsewhere. . . ."[5] What Bridges says of music could be well said for all of worship. If the worshipers only find in church what they find in the world outside the church—why come back?

Discover ways that you can draw the line between sacred and secular so that your people can discover, like Isaiah, some vision and awe that transcends the everyday.

Making the Connections

At the risk of contradiction, we now turn to the flip side. Each congregation must struggle long and hard to draw the line between sacred and secular. What happens in church should be different from what they find in the rest of the world.

At the same time, the worship of God can never be irrelevant, removed from life and the hurts of the world. Isaiah discovered that the Temple was *the* place where he connected his life with larger concerns. In the Temple, surrounded by the symbols of his faith, he saw himself as he was, he heard a Voice he heard no other place, and he was called to a life of service in the world.

Through every part of worship we must strive to link our ordinary life with our faith. None of this matters if we do not truly see. This seeing leads us to some understanding of self that is real and right. Such a seeing helps us discover a forgiveness that goes to the bedrock of our lives and leads us out beyond the stained-glass windows to change the world for Christ's sake.

Notes

1. Robert E. Webber, *Worship Is a Verb* (Waco, Texas: Word, Incorporated, 1985), 24.

2. *Ibid.*, 24.

3. David James Randolph, *God's Party* (Nashville: Abingdon, 1975), 72-73.

4. Lyle E. Schaller, *Survival Tactics in the Parish* (Nashville: Abingdon Press, 1977), 161.

5. Quoted in James Berry's *In the Beauty of Holiness* (privately printed by the Myers Park Baptist Church, Charlotte, North Carolina, 1986).

Postlude

The clock on the steeple under the cross chimes twelve times. The hour has passed quickly and church is over for another week. Ushers take their places at the doors. The choir has returned to the robing room. The pastor stands at the door, stooping to shake hands with a child, hugging Mrs. Jones in her mink. The nice-looking young couple trail by and move out into the sunlight. The old man with his cane wonders where he parked his car. In a few minutes the parking lot is empty and the pastor closes the doors, picks up his notes and Bible, and heads toward his car.

As he drives home he remembers something that Carlyle Marney said years before. He called it the churchmen's dream. Moving toward home, the pastor recalls the dream. On Monday morning when the custodians come in to sweep out the sanctuary from Sunday's service they will discover the strangest things. Instead of umbrellas, odd gloves, idly penciled notes, and discarded orders of service, they will come upon some other things. Scattered here and there they will find some big man's deep grief and another's disappointment and someone's sense of failure. They will stumble on some quiet woman's bitter hurt, another's painful pride, and someone's quarrel with God. Far over in another section, so tiny they almost miss it, they come upon some youngster's sin and they will find the bulky trash of someone's badly bruised ego, left behind where it belonged.

The pastor remembered the end of the dream. All that was found would be swept out and thrown away when church is over.[1] In the car, with no one but himself, the pastor mutters what only God Himself can hear: "This is what it is all about. This is what it is really all about."

Notes

1. Quoted in Frederick B. Speakman's *God and Jack Wilson* (Westwood, New Jersey: Fleming H. Revell Company, 1965), 98-99.

Discussion Guide for Sunday School Classes or Adult Retreats

The chapters in this book could easily be adapted for an 11-week course of study. The questions have been arranged so that they could be discussed in a group setting. Individuals who are worship leaders, like pastors, ministers of education, or music, might want to do these exercises individually. These questions could be used to lead your congregation in a study of worship on Sunday or Wednesday evenings. Some of the chapters could easily be studied in one session—baptism and the Lord's Supper might be combined. You might want to expand this study and spend several weeks on the first chapter.

Getting Ready

Before you begin your class, have members of your group interview your pastor or minister of music. Ask:

Who plans the worship services in our church?
What is supposed to happen as we worship God?
What do you, as a worship leader, hope to accomplish through the service?
Are there things we can do to prepare for worship?
What do you expect of us during the worship service?
How can we help to make worship a meaningful experience for our church?
Ask your pastor to tell you of the most moving worship experience he can remember.

Ask your church secretary for copies of your church

bulletins, Lord's Supper services, baptismal programs. Special programs like dedication services or ordination services will be helpful as you study the various chapters of this book. You might have one member of the group in charge of duplicating these orders of worship so that each person present can have a copy.

1. Rock or Sand?

In your first meeting share with the group your discussion with the pastor or minister of music. You might place their specific suggestions on a chalkboard or newsprint.

Now take your order of worship and study it carefully. This chapter has said there are four tests of authentic worship: 1) Biblical base; 2) Historical base; 3) Local base; 4) Strong artistic sensitivity. Point out the ways these principles are embedded in your church's worship guide.

In what ways does your service reflect 1) the ordered worship of our English heritage; 2) the frontier tradition? Explain.

What parts of the service reflect your own local setting and traditions? What do you like about these traditions? At what points would you say your service is beautiful? What moves you toward beauty in the service?

What changes would you make that would be helpful to you and to your congregation?

2. This Is the Word of God

You might begin this discussion by having the group share times when the Bible has come alive for them, personally, in a worship service. It might have been a hymn, drama, sermon, or stained glass that made the Scripture come alive. Share these experiences with the group. The leader might write these on newsprint or chalkboard.

Take your order of service and study the Scripture passages. Are Old and New Testaments included? What part

do the Psalms play in your order of worship? What scrip-
tural base does the music for the day play in your church?

Now select a biblical text. Take Psalm 23 or Luke 15:11-
24. Divide into two or three groups and select one of these
two Scriptures. Decide how this could be used effectively
in three different ways in your service. Call the group
back together and discuss.

3. Let Us Bow Our Heads

Take your bulletin and name the kinds of prayers you
find in your regular Sunday worship service. Write these
on the blackboard. Discuss the different kinds of prayers
you pray at church and why they are different.

Now give your group a theme like 1 Corinthians 13 or
Matthew 28:19-20. Ask each member to write different
types of prayers for one service using one theme. One
member would write a call to worship, another an invocation, another the morning prayer, another a confession,
an offertory prayer or a benediction. After these are written, share them with the group. You might have two
members take the prayers and arrange them into one service dealing with love or missions. Report on that structure, incorporating the classes' work at the start of your
next meeting.

4. A Faith that Sings

You might begin by letting two group members share
the prayers they have arranged in one service. Now take
the theme that you have just discussed and divide your
class into two groups. Let them pick music for the whole
service that can be used effectively. After they have
shared their suggestions, have them to study a regular
service of worship in your church.

Ask how does your church's music employ hymns, gospel songs, choruses, and contemporary music? How well
does your congregation sing? How does the music make

you feel? How is the music in your church different from what you hear in the world? Discuss. Share your findings with your minister of music.

5. Rabbits and Jesus

Pass out copies of your Sunday worship guide. Imagine that you are seven years old. What does your church provide in the worship service that can help you at this early age? Discuss. Now make suggestions of things that can be done that might make a seven-year-old experience the holy on Sunday morning.

Discuss the ways we learn found in chapter 5. Break into small groups and write a children's sermon that will incorporate more than the verbal.

End your session by having the group brainstorm other ways you might include little ones in your worship experience. Pass on these suggestions to your church staff.

6. How Can a Man Preach?

Recall the sermons you have heard. Which sermon can you remember that helped to change your life or alter your way of thinking? Discuss. Can you name anything about the delivery of the speaker that helped you with this change? Discuss.

What would you tell your pastor about his sermons that could help him? Name some great theme you would like to see addressed by your pastor.

Break into four groups. Write out a prayer for your pastor that lifts him up as a preacher. Come back into a circle and share these petitions. You might then give them to your minister.

7. Upon the Profession of Your Faith

Begin this session by asking the members of the group to remember their own baptism. How old were you? Were you scared? What instructions were you given? Was it

morning or evening? Who was the pastor? What stands
out most in that service?

Now break into three groups. You are to plan a baptismal service as part of the general worship service. After
you have planned this service, come back into the larger
group and discuss.

8. Lord's Supper

How often does your church observe the Lord's Supper?
Ask members of the group to think back on the Communion experiences of their lives. Ask them to discuss one
time when the Lord's Supper touched them in a meaningful way.

Break into three groups. Make sure these are not the
same people who were in last week's group. You want variety in their creativity. Take your church's order of worship for the Lord's Supper. With this as a guide, let your
group write their own service. Plan for much group participation. Share with the larger group when finished.

9. When Bushes Burn

Before the group begins ask your pastor if he can meet
with your group this week. Before the meeting ask him to
be prepared to discuss the special days in your church's
life for the last twelve months. He might want to photo-
copy special service programs and have them available as
he talks.

After he has discussed, have each member of your
group go around the circle and tell of a special service in
worship that they found meaningful. Have them explain
why they were touched in that particular service.

10. To Everything There Is a Season

This chapter dealt with weddings and funerals. Can
you remember a particular wedding that reflected a

Christian orientation? Discuss. Name ways that faith can shape our marriage ceremony.

Ask your group members to recall a funeral that was especially meaningful. This may even produce tears if they recall a family member's service. Do not be afraid of the emotion. Do not block the feelings of your group. Ask: What was it about that event that was uplifting?

Ask each one present to plan their own funeral service. Where would it be held? What part would music play? What would you want the pastor to say? What Scripture would you want used? What would you want included in that service that reflects a Christian orientation?

11. Hope for Years to Come

Begin your discussion by having your group open their Bibles to Isaiah 6:1-9. List the ways that Isaiah was a participant in that worship experience.

Now take last Sunday's worship program. Discuss the ways that your church provides for breaking out of the spectator trap. What suggestions would you offer to improve your church's participation?

Our tradition believes in the doctrine of the priesthood of all believers. How can this doctrine be implemented into your church's worship? Be positive and specific.

Discuss: 1) The ways words can be used meaningfully in your service. 2) Discuss the nonverbal ways that can help your congregation praise God. Be specific—no generalities.

Brainstorm the ways your worship leaders might help your congregation learn to worship more meaningfully. List these on a chalkboard or newsprint. Have some members discuss these suggestions with your pastor.

Draw a line down the chalkboard. On one side write "sacred," and on the other side write "secular." Now list those things that should be and not be in your church's worship experiences. Discuss.

Discuss how the church can make connection with the lives of the people. List ways the whole service (not just the sermon) can help make worship meaningful for your people.

End your last session with a prayer time. Ask members to pray sentence prayers about what you want to see happen as you gather for worship.

A Short Bibliography on Worship Structure

Abba, Raymond, *Principles of Christian Worship* (New York: Oxford University Press, 1966). Excellent guide to help you deal with the basic principles of Christian worship.

Dale, Robert D., *Keeping the Dream Alive* (Nashville: Broadman Press, 1988).

Dale, Robert D., *To Dream Again* (Nashville: Broadman Press, 1981). Both of Dale's books on long-range planning talk about ways that worship can be used to help you dream your dreams for the church of the future.

Doran, Carol and Thomas H. Troeger, *Open to Glory* (Valley Forge: Judson Press, 1983). A fine book that will help you explore your own creativity in worship planning. Excellent.

Horn, Henry E., *Worship in Crisis* (Philadelphia: Fortress Press, 1972). A book that explores some of the traps we fall into in worship and offers practical suggestions to help the worship planner.

L'Engle, Madeleine, *Walking on Water* (New York: Bantam Books, 1980). An excellent meditation on creativity.

Sparkman, G. Temp, *Writing Your Own Worship Materials* (Valley Forge: Judson Press, 1980). This is as practical a guide as I know to help the working pastor learn how to stretch his creativity in worship planning.

Webber, Robert E., *Worship Is a Verb* (Waco: TX: Word Books, 1985). Excellent from an Evangelical perspective.

Winward, S. F., *The Reformation of Our Worship* (Richmond, VA: John Knox Press, 1967). An excellent study for understanding the Evangelical Church in worship.

Willimon, William H., *The Service of God* (Nashville: Abingdon Press, 1983). A fine book that blends worship and pastoral care.

Bible

Barclay, William, *The Making of the Bible* (Nashville: Abingdon Press, 1961). Good introduction of how the Bible came to be.

Sanders, James, *Torah and Canon* (Philadelphia: Fortress Press, 1972). Excellent introduction showing how the canon came to be shaped.

Smart, James D., *The Strange Silence of the Bible in the Church* (Philadelphia: The Westminster Press, MCMLXX). A challenge to rediscovering the Bible in the church's work and worship.

Prayer

Appleton, George, ed., *The Oxford Book of Prayer* (New York: Oxford University Press, 1985) An excellent book that includes prayers of all types from all traditions.

Campbell, Ernest T., *Where Cross the Crowded Ways* (New York: Association Press, 1973). Good model for pastoral prayers.

Ferris, Thomas Parker, *Prayers* (New York: The Seabring Press, 1981). A great book of prayers for the church written by a master craftsman.

Killinger, John, *Lost in Wonder, Love & Praise* (Lynchburg, VA: Angel Books, 1986). A fine compilation of prayers for all of worship, written by a pastor.

Phillips, Lee, *Breaking Silence Before the Lord* (Grand Rapids, MI: Baker Book House, 1986). This book will help the working pastor stretch his creativity with a multitude of prayer forms.

Phillips, Lee, *Prayers for Our Day* (Atlanta: John Knox Press, 1982). Beautifully written prayers that will be helpful for your own devotional life and models for public prayers.

Phillips, Lee, *Prayers for Worship* (Waco, TX: Word Books, 1979).

Music

Bailey, Albert Edward, *The Gospel in Hymns* (New York: Charles Scribner's Sons, 1950). A classic dealing with stories behind the great hymns of the faith.

Eskew, Harry and Hugh T. McElrath, *Sing With Understanding* (Nashville: Broadman Press, 1980). Excellent and practical.

Hustad, Donald P., *Jubilate!* (Carol Stream, IL.: Hope Publishing Company, 1981).

Ray, James D., compiler, *The Hymnal* (North Charleston, S.C. 29406: Soft Ray Resources, P.O. Box 5345, 1987). This is a valuable reference book which indexes hymns, hymn tunes, Scripture references, and key words in six popular evangelical hymnals.

Reynolds, William J., *Companion to Baptist Hymnal* (Nashville: Broadman Press, 1976). Most of the hymns in the *Baptist Hymnal* come alive as Reynolds explains how they came to be.

Routley, Erik, *Church Music and the Christian Faith* (Carol Stream, IL.: Agape, 1978). A standard text for those interested in church music.

Wren, Brian, has published two collections of new hymns which might prove very helpful. *Faith Looking Forward* and *Praising a Mystery* (Carol Stream, IL.: Hope Publishing Company, 1983, 1986). Recommended highly.

Wohlgemuth, Paul W., *Rethinking Church Music* (Carol Stream, IL.: Hope Publishing Company, 1981). Excellent book for those who want to study music in the

Evangelical tradition.

Hymnals Which Might Prove Helpful

Hymns for the Living Church, Donald P. Hustad, ed. (Carol Stream, IL.: Hope Publishing Company, 1974).

Rejoice in the Lord, Erik Routley, ed. (Grand Rapids: Wm. B. Eerdmans Publishing Company, 1985). This book, edited by a master of hymnody, will introduce you to many new hymns written today as well as introduce you to some of the great hymns of the church.

Songs of Fellowship, Book One (Lottbridge Drove, Eastbourne, E. Sussex BN23 6NT: Kingsway Publications, 1984).

Songs of Fellowship, Box Three (E. Sussex, BN23 6NT: Kingsway Publications, 1985). These books will give you some understanding of choruses which many churches are singing. Many of these are excellent.

The Baptist Hymn Book (London: Psalms and Hymns Trust, 4 Southhampton Row, W.C. 1, 1978). This British Baptist hymnbook is a wonderful compilation of many of the great hymns that British Baptists enjoy.

The Oxford Book of Carols, Percy Dearmer, R. Vaughan Williams, Martin Shaw, ed. (Oxford: Oxford University Press, 1964). This book is a classic of Christmas carols.

Children's Sermons

Coleman, Richard, *Gospel-Telling* (Grand Rapids: William B. Eerdmans Publishing Company, 1982). This resource book is excellent in explaining how children learn and helping the Pastor give substance to this time in worship.

Fowler, James W., *Stages of Faith* (San Francisco: Harper and Row, 1981). An understanding of Fowler's stages will help any person as they communicate with children and adults.

Hendricks, William L., *A Theology for Children* (Nashville: Broadman Press, 1980). Excellent in dealing with how children can learn about God.

Preaching

Barry, James C., *Preaching in Today's World* (Nashville: Broadman Press, 1984). This book is an excellent compilation of some of the best preaching in Southern Baptist pulpits.

Buechner, Frederick, *Telling the Truth* (San Francisco: Harper & Row, Publishers, 1977). These Lyman Beecher Lectures are a great addition for the preacher who would like to study the craft.

Cox, James W., ed., *Best Sermons 1* (San Francisco: Harper & Row, Publishers, 1988).

Cox, James W., ed., *Best Sermons 2* (San Francisco: Harper & Row, Publishers, 1989). These two volumes offer some of the best illustrations of preaching that we have today.

Scherer, Paul E., *The Word God Sent* (San Francisco: Harper & Row, Publishers, 1965). This book has been reprinted by Baker Book House under the title, *The Word of God Sent*. Though the book came out some 20 years ago, it is a book of theory and practice by a great pulpiteer.

Preaching Journals

Biblical Preaching Journal, Gary Kidwell, ed., P. O. Box 23557, Lexington, KY 40523. This periodical follows the Lectionary and is edited by a Disciple of Christ minister. The working pastor will find sermons from ministers of all denominations. Most helpful.

Journal for Preachers, T. Erskine Clark and Tom G. Long, eds., published quarterly, Box 520, Decatur, GA 30031-0520. Excellent resource for the pastor.

Pulpit Digest, David Farmer, ed. (Published by Harper &

Row, Publishers, P. O. Box 1537, Hagerstown, MD
21741). Published bimonthly and is most helpful for the
preacher.
Selected Sermons (Episcopal Church Center, 815 Second
Avenue, New York, NY 10017). This sermon series is
published by the Episcopal Church but invites ministers of all denominations to write. Good resource.

Baptism

Willimon, William H., *Remember Your Baptism* (Nashville: The Upper Room, 1980). This book, written by a
Methodist, gives some solid background material on
early baptismal practices.
Willimon, William H., *Word, Water, Wine and Bread*
(Valley Forge: Judson Press, 1980). This book is a good
resource on worship in general and has some excellent
historical information of baptismal practices in early
church history.

Lord's Supper

Willimon, William H., *Word, Water, Wine, and Bread*
(Valley Forge: Judson Press, 1980). This book has a
splendid section on the Lord's Supper as well as general
worship information.
Willimon, William H., *Sunday Dinner* (Nashville: The
Upper Room, 1981). You will find some historical information about the Lord's Supper but you will also discover some excellent devotional material concerning
the Supper. Excellent source book.

Special Days

Aldridge, Marion D., *The Pastor's Guidebook, A Manual
for Special Occasions* (Nashville: Broadman Press,
1989). This working pastor has written an excellent
guide to help the minister as he plans for special days.

Christensen, James L., *Creative Ways to Worship* (Old Tappan, NJ: Fleming H. Revell Company, 1974).

Christensen, James L., *New Ways to Worship* (Old Tappan, NJ: Fleming H. Revell Company, 1973). These two volumes have a multitude of ideas that will prove helpful as you plan for special occasions in worship.

Gulledge, Jack, ed. *Sermons and Services for Special Days* (Nashville: Convention Press, 1979). This booklet has many excellent resources for helping the minister as he prepares for special occasions.

Payne, Ernest A., and Stephen F. Winward, *Orders and Prayers for Church Worship* (London: The Carey Kingsgate Press, 1962). Though this book is out of print, it provides helpful information for all sorts of services we engage in.

Weddings and Funerals

Mace, David and Vera, *How to Have a Happy Marriage* (Nashville: Abingdon Press, 1977). Excellent book that will help any working pastor as he counsels those planning to be married.

Rest, Frederick, *Funeral Handbook* (Valley Forge: Judson Press, 1982). An excellent loose-leaf book that the pastor can take to the funeral service that has many resources of Scriptures and helps for the funeral.

Trueblood, Elton, *The Common Ventures of Life* (New York: Harper & Row, Publishers, 1949) A fine book that deals with religious dimensions of marriage, birth, work, and death.

Appendix
(Worship Services)

Psalm Service

This whole service is an example of one way you might use the whole of the Psalter in one worship hour to teach a deeper love and understanding of the types of psalms.

Morning Worship

Dietrich Bonhoeffer, the martyred Christian whose writings have profoundly influenced contemporary theology, regarded the Psalter as his favorite book in the Bible. His last publication before his execution by the Nazis was *The Prayer Book of the Bible: An Introduction to the Psalms* (1940). In this pamphlet he developed the view that just as Jesus Christ has taught us to pray the words of the Lord's Prayer, so "the prayer book of the Bible" contains in greater fullness and richness the words which God wants us to speak to Him in the name of Jesus Christ. He argued that it is proper, therefore, for the New Testament and the Psalms to be bound together; for, as one of his interpreters, John Godsey, puts it, "it is the prayer of the church of Jesus Christ and belongs to the Lord's Prayer."

The Prelude....."The Lord's My Shepherd"....... Haan
(Based on Psalm 23, Psalm of Trust)
The Chiming of the Hour .... Ms. Skinner

The Call to Worship....."Praise the Lord" CARPENTER
1970
(Based on Psalm 113:1,2; Psalm of Praise)
The Invocation and Lord's Prayer .... Rev. Hobart
The Hymn of Praise, #11....."Praise the Lord! Ye Heavens, Adore Him" .... HYFRYDOL
(Based on Psalm 148, Psalm of Praise)
The Welcome .... Rev. Hobart
The Time of Giving.................... Congregation
The Offertory....."Praise to the Lord, the Almighty" arr.
Phillips
(Based on Psalms 103 & 150; Psalms of Praise)
The Doxology .... Congregation
(OLD 100TH Psalm tune, Psalm of Praise)
Children will leave for Junior Church.
The Offertory Prayer .... Ms. Cecilia Hartsell
The Scripture Lesson.....Psalm 66:5-12.... Ms. Hartsell
(Psalm of Praise)
Sermon.....THREE KINDS OF PRAYERS..... Dr. Lovette
Invitation to the Table................ Dr. Lovette
Prayer of Confession .. Dr. Lovette and Congregation
Leader: Have mercy upon me, O God, according to Thy
steadfast love;
People: According to Thy abundant mercy blot out my
transgressions,
Leader: Wash me thoroughly from my iniquity,
People: And cleanse me from my sin!
(Ps. 51:1-2, Individual Lament).

The Bread

People: " ... they had no faith in God, and did not trust
his saving power. Yet he commanded the skies
above, and opened the doors of heaven; and he
rained down upon them manna to eat, and gave
them the grain of heaven"
(Ps. 78:22-24, Salvation History Psalm).

Prayer for the Bread .... Mr. Joe Turner
Hymn for the Bread, #163....."Rock of Ages, Cleft for
Me"..................................... TOPLADY
(Based on Ps. 94:22, Community Lament.)
The congregation and choir will sing all stanzas

The Cup

People: "He cleft rocks in the wilderness, and gave them
        drink abundantly as from the deep. He made
        streams come out of the rock and caused waters
        to flow down like rivers"
        (Ps. 78:15-16, Salvation History Psalm).
Prayer for the Cup .... Mrs. Winnie Williams
Meditation for the Cup....."A Hymn of Supplication"
.... McAfee
(Based on Ps. 51, Individual Lament)

O Lord have mercy now we pray, and save us by Thy stead-
    fast love,
For we have wandered from Thy way: forgive us from above.
Against Thee only do we sin, and we are helpless in Thy
    sight;
Without Thee all is dark within: Lord lead us by Thy light.
Create within us clean hearts, and fashion spirits fresh and
    new;
Restore the joy Thy love imparts: Lord, keep us strong and
    true. Amen

Hymn of Fellowship, #282....."Jesus Shall Reign Wher-
e'er the Sun" .... DUKE STREET
(Based on Ps. 72, Royal Psalm)
The Reception of New Members .... Congregation
The Church Notices .... Dr. Lovette
The Choral Benediction..."All People that on Earth Do
Dwell" .... Congregation and Choir
(Based on Ps. 100, Psalm of Praise)

The Lord, ye know, is God indeed,

Without our aid he did us make;
We are his folk, he doth us feed,
And for his sheep he doth us take. Amen.

The Postlude....."Rejoice, Ye Pure in Heart" arr. Jordan
(Based on Ps. 20, Royal Psalm)
Concerning Today's Worship Service—Our entire Communion service this morning is built around the Psalms. Dr. Lovette will speak on the Psalms in a sermon entitled "Three Kinds of Prayers." He will talk about three different kinds of psalms that we find in the Psalter. They are 1) Psalms of Lamentation; 2) Psalms of Thanksgiving; 3) Psalms of Worship and Praise. We will use different hymns this morning that will reflect the different kinds of psalms. The choral and instrumental music is all taken from the texts of the Psalter. All Scripture passages will also be from the Psalms. It is our hope and prayer that this service will deepen your love for this great body of biblical literature.

Service on Prayer

This worship service incorporated the different kinds of prayers that the church prays in worship and explained them. All the hymns and music were related to the theme of prayer.

Morning Worship

Because we cannot reasonably expect to erect a constantly expanding structure of social activism upon a constantly diminishing foundation of faith, attention to the cultivation of the inner life is our first order of business, even in a period of rapid social change. The Church, if it is to affect the world, must become a center from which new spiritual power emanates. While the Church must be secular in the sense that it operates in the world, if it is only secular it will not have the desired effect upon the secular order which it is called upon to penetrate. With no diminution of concern for people, we can and must give new attention to the production of a trustworthy religious experience.

—Elton Trueblood

We Come To Worship

The Prelude....."Priere A Notre-Dame"...... Boellman
The Chiming of the Hour .... Mr. Breazeale
The Call to Worship....."Lord, Teach Us How to Pray Aright" .... ST. AGNES
The Invocation (We ask God to be with us) Mr. McDade
The Lord's Prayer............ Congregation and Choir
(Uniting us with the church of the ages)
Our Father, which art in heaven, Hallowed be thy name. Thy kingdom come. Thy will be done in earth as it is in heaven. Give us this day our daily bread. And forgive us our debts, as we forgive our debtors. And lead us not into temptation, but deliver us from evil: For thine is the kingdom, and the power, and the glory, for ever. Amen.

We Praise God

The Hymn of Praise, #13...."Come, Thou Fount of Every Blessing"............................ NETTLETON
The Welcome to Worshipers............. Mr. McDade
The Scripture Lesson.....Psalm 108:1-5.... Mr. McDade
The Prayer of Confession .... Mr. McDade and
Congregation
(We confess the wrongs we have committed)
Leader: We come to confess to You, Lord.
People: We are not the persons we would like others to think we are.
Leader: We are not the persons we would like to think of ourselves as being.

People: Only in the security of Your love are we able to admit our secret fears and desires.

Leader: Hear them now, O Lord, and forgive us for every deception. (Pause) Give us new life from above and reshape us in the image of Christ, for we pray in His special name. Amen.

—John Killinger (adapted)

Words of Absolution.................... Mr. McDade
(We receive the forgiveness God offers)

He was wounded for our transgressions and bruised for our iniquities. The Lord has laid on Him the chastisement of our peace and by His stripes we are healed. Therefore, God forgives us all of every hurt, every wrong, and every broken place in our lives. Amen.

Intercessory Prayer (We pray for others) . Congregation
For these we pray: Henry Stover, Leslie Kearns, Bob Davis, Chris Rochester, Richard Wilkey, Geneva Lawless, the family of Evelyn Boykin, the world Christ loves

Silent Prayer (We pray for our personal concerns)
.... Congregation

Pastoral Prayer........................ Dr. Lovette
(The pastor prays for the needs of thecongregation and world)

We Bring Our Gifts

Hymn of Giving, #358....."Open My Eyes that I May See" .... SCOTT

Offertory....."Speak, Lord, in the Stillness"Green/Hustad

Doxology (A prayer of praise and thanksgiving)
.... Congregation

Offertory Prayer .... Mrs. Sheila Lynn
(We thank God for the good gifts of our lives and the constancy of His grace)

We Hear God's Word

Children's Time........................ Rev. Hobart

Solo....."If My People Will Pray".............. Owens
Ann Summers Perkins, soprano
The Sermon.....WAYS TO STRENGTHEN YOUR PRAYER LIFE
.... Dr. Lovette

We Make Our Commitment

The Hymn of Commitment, #213...."Savior, Like a Shep-
herd Lead Us"........................ BRADBURY
The Reception of New Members......... Congregation
The Church Notices...................... Dr. Lovette
The Benediction (A prayer for parting).... Dr. Lovette
The Choral Benediction....."O Master, Let Me Walk with
Thee"................................ MARYTON
The Postlude....."Fanfare on Heavenly Sunlight". Cook

Service on World Hunger

This service is an example of how you might engage
your congregation in the subject of world hunger, using a
thematic approach.

Morning Worship

My name is Gunnet. My four children and I live in
the Tigray province of Ethiopia. My husband was
killed in one of the battles between the government
and the Tigray Liberation Front. We have been poor
as long as I can remember, but this drought...it gets
worse and worse. This past year it has been all I
could do just to keep my children alive. I can't feed
my baby anymore, my milk has dried up because I
can't get enough to eat. My son has been sick with
malaria. If only he had enough food to eat he could
fight off the infection. I am thankful we live close to
a road. It is only a ten-hour walk to a spot where food
is delivered. For others it is much longer. I pray for
those who live too far from the road to get help.
Sometimes we sit for days waiting for the food to arrive. They say there are not enough trucks to deliver

the food so we never know when it will come. Every night I wonder if I will have four children in the morning. Each one is so special, but I feel helpless to save them.

—from Bread for the World Fact Sheet

We Come To Worship

The Prelude....."He Leadeth Me" .. Debra Fagan, piano
The Chiming of the Hour . . . . Mrs. Halfacre
The Spoken Call to Worship. . . . . Rev. Hobart
We come to this World Hunger Sunday to remember that members of our family are dying. Children are dying of hunger. They, like us, are the body of Christ. Worldwide 40,000 children die each day of hunger. One child every six seconds. Children just like our own. One child every six seconds. In 24 African nations 150 million people, most of them children, God's children, are without enough food; they are hungry. Many will die of hunger today. One child every six seconds. One of God's children.
The Invocation and Lord's Prayer . . . . Rev. Hobart and
Congregation
Help us, oh Lord, to listen to You, to be Your instruments, to feed the hungry, to act without selfishness, to love others as ourselves. Help us, oh Lord, as parents help their children, to accept our commonality with all Your children around the world. Help us, oh Lord, to know what to do. Move us from contemplation to action, in keeping with Your will. Help us now to genuinely pray together the prayer Your Son, Jesus, gave us.

We Praise God

The Hymn of Praise, #11....."Praise the Lord!"
. . . . HYFRYDOL
The Welcome to Visitors and Church Notices
. . . . Dr. Lovette

The Scripture Lesson, Response #597... Rev. Hall and
Congregation
The Morning Prayer...................... Rev. Hall
We Bring Our Gifts

The Hymn of Giving, #409....."When We Walk with the
Lord"......................... TRUST AND OBEY
The Offertory....."The Day Thou Gavest"ST. CLEMENT
The Presentation of Gifts.............. Congregation

> Kum ba yah, my Lord, Kum ba yah! Kum ba yah,
> my Lord, kum ba yah!
> Kum ba yah, my Lord, Kum ba yah!
> O Lord, Kum ba yah.
> Someone's hungry Lord, Kum ba yah (repeat)
> Come by here, Lord, come by here! (repeat)

The Offertory Prayer........... Mrs. Frances Rostron
The Children's Time.................... Rev. Hobart

We Hear God's Word

The Anthem....."The Eyes of All Wait Upon Thee"Berger
The Sermon.....JESUS AND THE POOR......... Rev. Hall
The Hymn of Commitment, #341....."The Lord's My
Shepherd"............................. CRIMOND
The Reception of New Members........ Congregation
The Benediction....................... Dr. Lovette
The Choral Benediction....."Amen".......... Telemann
The Postlude....."O For a Thousand Tongues". AZMON

Service from Galatians Series

Here is an example of how one service in a series can
implement the biblical theme throughout the whole service. This service begins with baptism.

Morning Worship

> O my God, thou art very near, in my heart and
> about my way; yet often thou dost seem very far off

and my soul fainteth for looking after thee: thou dost lead me through dark places and withdrawest thyself from me. In the desolate time, when I feel perplexed and forsaken, I would think upon the cross of my Saviour and his dreadful cry, that my faith may hold fast in his faith and that despair may not seize me. Help me to remember the days of vision and sure confidence, guide me to stay my soul in the revelations of thyself which thou hast given me in time past through all thy prophets and servants, and bring me out of the valley of the dark shade once more into the light of thy presence, through Jesus Christ our Lord.—W. R. Matthews, 1881-1973

We Come to Worship

The Prelude.....'"Blessed Jesus, At Thy Word".... Ahle
The Chiming of the Hour .... Mr. Breazeale
The Call to Worship....."Come, Be Baptized" .... Smith
The Invocation and Lord's Prayer .... Mr. McDade

We Praise God

The Service of Baptism

Lea Knight   Nic Noblet   Sarah Wilkey
(After each candidate is baptized, the congregation will sing one stanza of "Come, Thou Fount of Every Blessing.")

> 1. Come, thou Fount of ev'ry blessing,
>   Tune my heart to sing thy grace;
>   Streams of mercy, never ceasing,
>   Call for songs of loudest praise:
>   Teach me some melodious sonnet,
>   Sung by flaming tongues above;
>   Praise the mount! I'm fixed upon it,
>   Mount of thy redeeming love.
> 2. Here I raise mine Ebenezer;
>   Hither by thy help I'm come;

And I hope, by thy good pleasure,
Safely to arrive at home:
Jesus sought me when a stranger,
Wand'ring from the fold of God;
He, to rescue me from danger,
Interposed his precious blood.
3. O to grace how great a debtor
Daily I'm constrained to be!
Let thy grace, Lord, like a fetter,
Bind my wand'ring heart to thee:
Prone to wander, Lord, I feel it,
Prone to leave the God I love;
Here's my heart, Lord, take and seal it,
Seal it for thy courts above.

The Prayer for the Candidates and for Us All
.... Mr. McDade
The Welcome to Worshipers............. Mr. McDade
The Scripture Lesson.....Galatians 5:16-26
.... Mr. McDade
The Call to Confession................. Mr. McDade
The Silent Prayer..................... Congregation
The Assurance of Pardon.....Galatians 6:9-10
.... Mr. McDade
The Morning Prayer .... Mr. McDade
The Presentation to the Baptismal Candidates
.... Mr. Butch Trent
The Laying on of Hands .... The Church
    (At this time deacons, staff members, parents, and Sunday School teachers are encouraged to come forward and set these new believers apart for Christian service.)

We Bring Our Gifts

The Offertory....."Jesu, Joy of Man's Desiring"Pachelbel
The Doxology .... Congregation
        (Children will leave for Junior Church.)
The Offertory Prayer................ Dr. Ray Noblet

We Hear God's Words

The Solo....."Help Us Accept Each Other"....Beck
Lynne King, soprano
The Sermon.....THE ART OF HANGING IN THERE..... Dr.
Lovette

We Make Our Commitment

The Hymn of Commitment, #383....."How Firm a
Foundation"........................ FOUNDATION
The Reception of New Members......... Congregation
The Church Notices.................... Dr. Lovette
The Benediction........................ Dr. Lovette
The Choral Response....."A Blessing".......... Bennett
The Postlude....."Maestoso" .... Heger

Service on Hebrews

Here is another example of using one service in a series
to help your congregation deal with the biblical text for
the day.

Morning Worship

Be this the central faith and fact of life: that there
is a light beyond our darkness, and a purpose which
makes music of our confusion—and we, you, and I
have some part in both. Hold fast to that and fear
nothing.
—Gerald Bullett

We Come to Worship

The Prelude .... "Trumpet Dialogue/Kyrie"
.... Clerambault/Couperin
The Chiming of the Hour .... Ms. Halfacre
The Call to Worship.................... Rev. Hobart
Leader: Since we are surrounded by so great a cloud of

witnesses, let us also lay aside every weight, and
sin which clings so closely,
People: And let us run with perseverance the race that
is set before us,
Leader: Looking to Jesus the pioneer and perfecter of
our faith, who for the joy that was set before him
endured the cross, despising the shame, and is
seated at the right hand of the throne of God.
People: Consider him who endured from sinners such
hostility against himself, so that you may not
grow weary or fainthearted (Heb. 12:1-3).
The Invocation and Lord's Prayer   Rev. Hobart

We Praise God

The Hymn of Praise, #43........ "All Praise to Thee"
.... SINE NOMINE
The Welcome to Visitors................ Rev. Hobart
The Scripture Lesson................... Dr. Lovette

Now faith is the assurance of things hoped for, the
conviction of things not seen. For by it the men of old
received divine approval.

By faith Noah, being warned by God concerning
events as yet unseen, took heed and constructed an
ark for the saving of his household.

By faith Abraham obeyed when he was called to go
out to a place which he was to receive as an inheri-
tance; and he went out, not knowing where he was to
go.

By faith Moses, when he was grown up, refused to
be called the son of Pharaoh's daughter, choosing
rather to share ill-treatment with the people of God
than to enjoy the fleeting pleasures of sin.

And what more shall I say? For time would fail me
to tell of Gideon. Barak, Samson, Jephthah, of David
and Samuel and the prophets—

Who through faith conquered kingdoms, enforced

justice, received promises, stopped the mouths of li-
ons, quenched raging fire, escaped the edge of the
sword.

Others suffered mocking and scourging, and even
chains and imprisonment.

They were stoned, they were sawn in two, they
were killed with the sword; they went about in skins
of sheep and goats, destitute, afflicted, ill-treated—of
whom the world was not worthy.

Therefore, since we are surrounded by so great a
cloud of witnesses, let us also lay aside every weight,
and sin which clings so closely.

And let us run with perseverance the race that is
set before us, looking to Jesus the pioneer and perfecter of our faith (Heb. 11— 12).

The Silent Prayer . . . . Congregation
The Pastoral Prayer . . . . Dr. Lovette

We Bring Our Gifts

The Hymn of Giving, #390 . . . . "O For a Faith"
. . . . ARLINGTON
The Offertory "How Fair and How Pleasant Art Thou"
. . . . Marcel Dupre
The Presentation of Gifts . . . . . . "God Forgave My Sin"
. . . . Congregation

> God forgave my sin in Jesus' name.
>   I've been born again in Jesus' name.
>   And in Jesus' name I come to you
>   To share his love as he told me to.
>   (Refrain)
> All power is giv'n in Jesus' name
>   In earth and heaven in Jesus' name.
>   And in Jesus' name I come to you
>   To share his pow'r as he told me to.
> (Refrain)
>   He said freely, freely you have received;
>   Freely, freely give.

Go in my name and because you believe,
Others will know that I live. Amen.

The Offertory Prayer................. Mrs. Mary Bell
The Children's Time.................... Mr. Hobart

We Hear God's Word

The Anthem....."Begin, My Soul"........ Shaw-Parker
The Sermon .... THE DISCIPLINE OF PERSEVERANCE
.... Dr. Lovette

We Make Our Response

The Hymn of Commitment, #265"God of Grace and God
of Glory"
.... CWM RHONDDA
The Reception of New Members .... Congregation
The Church Notices .... Dr. Lovette
The Benediction....................... Dr. Lovette
The Choral Response .... Sanctuary Choir
The Postlude....."Agincourt Hymn" ... John Dunstable

Service on Christmas Stories

This service used during our Advent celebration shows
how one may implement the Advent wreath with the text
for the day and how the whole service clusters around the
Mary story.

Morning Worship

She struck the angel Gabriel as hardly old enough
to have a child at all, let alone this child, but he'd
been entrusted with a message to give her, and he
gave it.

He told her what the child was to be named, and
who he was to be, and something about the mystery
that was to come upon her. "You mustn't be afraid,
Mary," he said.

As he said it, he only hoped she wouldn't notice

that beneath the great, golden wings he himself was trembling with fear to think that the whole future of creation hung now on the answer of a girl.
—See Luke 1:26-35.

The Prelude.....“Now Sing We, Now Rejoice”..... Manz
The Chiming of the Hour .... Mrs. Gaddis
The Lighting of the Advent Candles.................
                    The Charles Helsel Family
The Scripture: In the sixth month the angel Gabriel was sent from God to a city of Galilee named Nazareth, to a virgin betrothed to a man whose name was Joseph, of the house of David; and the virgin's name was Mary. And he came to her and said, 'Hail, O favored one, the Lord is with you!' But she was greatly troubled at the saying, and considered in her mind what sort of greeting this might be. And the angel said to her, 'Do not be afraid, Mary, for you have found favor with God. And behold, you will conceive in your womb and bear a son, and you shall call his name Jesus. He will be great, and will be called the Son of the Most High; and the Lord God will give to him the throne of his father David, and he will reign over the house of Jacob for ever and of his kingdom there will be no end (Luke 1:26-33).
The Meditation: Today we light two Advent candles. We are at midpoint in our Advent journey. As the messenger came to Mary, promising more than she ever imagined, may we too, discover for ourselves this holy season the best Christmas present ever.

The Advent Anthem....."E'en So, Lord Jesus, Quickly Come" .... Manz
The Invocation and Lord's Prayer .... Dr. Lovette
The Hymn of Praise, #79....."Come, Thou Long-Expected Jesus"................................. HYFRYDOL
The Welcome to Visitors and Church Notices ....
.... Dr. Lovette
The Scripture.....Luke 2:1-7.............. Dr. Beckett
The Silent Prayer .... Congregation
The Pastoral Prayer................... Dr. Beckett
The Hymn of Giving, #85....."O Little Town of Bethlehem".................................... ST. LOUIS
The   Offertory   Solo....."Sweet   Little   Jesus   Boy"
.... Traditional
                    Kim Fowler, soloist
The Presentation of Gifts .... Congregation

> Joy to the earth! the Savior reigns;
> Let men their songs employ;
> While fields and floods, rocks, hills, and plains,
>
> Repeat the sounding joy, Repeat the sounding joy;
> Repeat, repeat the sounding joy.

Offertory Prayer .... Mr. John Crow
The Children's Time.................... Dr. Lovette
The Anthem.............. "O Come, All Ye Faithful"
.... arr. Shaw-Bennett
The Sermon....."MARY'S STORY".............. Lovette
The Hymn of Commitment, #437....."Tell Me the Story of Jesus"......................... STORY OF JESUS
The Reception of New Members .... Congregation
The Benediction....................... Dr. Lovette
The Choral Benediction....."Be Near Me, Lord Jesus"
.... MUELLER

The Postlude.....'Sortie' .... Blake

Service of Baptism

This baptismal service was held on a Sunday evening. Here is an example where you might use your whole service to focus on the ordinance of Christian baptism.

Evening Worship

The Particular Baptist Confession of 1644 says baptism is important because: "First, the washing the whole soul in the blood of Christ; secondly, that interest the saints have in the death, burial, and resurrection; thirdly, together with a confirmation of our faith, that as certainly as the body is buried under water and riseth again, so certainly shall the bodies of the saints be raised by the power of Christ in the day of the resurrection, to reign with Christ."
—Ernest A. Payne

Prelude
Call to Worship
  Leader: Baptism is a symbol for beginning again.
  People: Behold, God makes all things new.
  Leader: Baptism is a symbol for dying.
  People: We die to all that which is old.
  Leader: Baptism is a symbol for living.
  People: We are resurrected to a new life in Christ Jesus.
  Leader: Baptism is symbolized with water.
  People: We are washed whiter than snow by Jesus' shed blood.
  Leader: Baptism is symbolized by total immersion.
  People: All of life is affected by what we do here tonight.
Hymn #387 .... "Jesus, I My Cross Have Taken"
Invocation .... Virgil Quisenberry

Hymn #188 . . . . Amazing Grace
Scripture Lesson . . . . Matthew 9:13-17; John 3:5-8

The Baptism of Believers

Introduction of the Candidates . . . . Dr. Lovette

Kim Atkinson	Britney Camper
Kendra Cover	Trey Dobey
Ashleigh Ford	Lee Hays
Missey McClain	Thomas Quisenberry

A word about Baptism . . . . Dr. Lovette
The Confession of the Candidates
The Laying on of Hands
(At this time the church is asked to come forward and
to lay hands on the candidates, setting them aside for
the service of God.)
The Dedicatory Prayer . . . . Peggy Cover
The Solo . . . . . . "Now I Belong to Jesus" . . . (arr. Bennett)
Lynda Willis, soprano

The Service of Baptism

(After each candidate is baptized, the congregation
will alternately sing the following choruses:)

Happy day, happy day, when Jesus washed my sins away!
He taught me how to watch and pray,
and live rejoicing every day.
Happy day, happy day, when Jesus washed my sins away!

Trust and obey, for there's no other way
To be happy in Jesus, but to trust and obey.

The Presentation of Bibles, Crosses, and Certificates
. . . . Winnie Williams
The Benediction. . . . . Danny Ford
The Postlude
Welcome Visitors—We welcome all visitors who wor-
ship with us on this special occasion. Please know that

we appreciate your presence and hope you will worship with us again at your next opportunity.

Parent-Child Dedication Service

Here is an order of worship for a Parent-Child Dedication Service. The theme of the whole service on Mother's Day was family, children, and parental responsibilities.

Morning Worship

A family is a group of people who actively approve of each other.... A family is a center of healing ... a place where you can live on a basis of being real, and recover your ability to be your honest self.... A family is an association of growers ... people growing simultaneously. So that a change in the fortunes of one affects all.... A family is a power center ... generating within its adults and children the love power so desperately needed in our world.... A family is communicated experience ... and the interpretation of it.... A family home is a center where lives are woven into the fabric of humanity.... A family home is a perpetual invitation to future.... A family is a colony of democracy.... All this is possible only when a family is looking together in the same direction ... toward God.

—Ross Snyder

The Prelude....."Today God's Only-Gotten Son" .. Bach
The Chiming of the Hour .... Mrs. Halfacre
The Choral Call to Worship.."Praise, My Soul, the King of Heaven"......................... LAUDA ANIMA
The Invocation and Lord's Prayer .... Mrs. Candy Bell
The Hymn of Praise, #143.... "Faith of Our Parents"
.... SAINT CATHERINE
(Insert the word, "parents" in the place of "fathers.")
The Welcome to Visitors................ Dr. Lovette

The Scripture Lesson, Response #607.....(1 Cor. 13) Mrs.
Susan Bass
The Service of Dedication for Parents and Children
  Maura Jeanne Capps, daughter of Mr. & Mrs. Kerry
Capps
  John Wright Coleman, son of Mr. & Mrs. Steve
Coleman
  Andrea Jane Crowe, daughter of Mr. & Mrs. David
Crowe
  Annie Laurie Esler, daughter of Mr. & Mrs. Harold
Esler
  David Matthew Peyton, son of Mr. & Mrs. Barry
Peyton
  Andrea Caroline Young, daughter of Mr. & Mrs.
Roy Young
The Naming of Our Commitments.... Dr. Lovette and
Parents

Pastor: Parents, why have you come?
Parents: To dedicate ourselves and our children to the
Lord.
Pastor: What do you hold in your arms?
Parents: God's gift of love in human flesh, breathing His
Spirit, bearing our name.
Pastor: What do you hold in your minds?
Parents: Visions of responsible parenthood, maturing
children, a Christian home, under our name.
Pastor: What do you hold in your hearts?
Parents: A prayer for wisdom, a hunger for righteous-
ness, a commitment to rear our children in the
nurture and admonition of the Lord . . . for His
Name's sake.
Parents: Community of the redeemed, how do you re-
spond to these affirmations?
Church: We will pray with you and for you. We will un-
dergird you in sorrow and happiness. We will
seek to live worthy of the ideals you aspire for

your children.

Pastor: Let the children lead us then, as God intended, to deeper faith and greater joy.

All: In the Name that is above every Name, Jesus Christ, our Lord, Amen. (E. Lee Phillips)

The Pledge of the Parents

The Prayer of Commitment . . . . Dr. Lovette

The Benediction for the Children . . . . Dr. Lovette

The Presentation of Certificates . . . . Dr. Lovette

The Solo.....ʺFor The Beauty of the Earthʺ . arr. Rutter
Jennifer Dubose, soloist

The Children's Sermon . . . . Mrs. Becky Jo Clark

The Offertory Anthem ʺThe Church's One Foundationʺ
. . . . AURELIA

The Doxology . . . . Congregation

The Offertory Prayer . . . . Mrs. Joanne Arbena

The Sermon.....VALUES TO LIVE BY . . . . Dr. Lovette

The Hymn of Commitment. . . . . ʺO God In Heavenʺ
. . . . MELITA

The Reception of New Members . . . . Congregation

The Church Notices . . . . Dr. Lovette

The Benediction. . . . . Dr. Lovette

The Choral Benediction. . . . . ʺAlleluiaʺ
. . . . LASST UNS ERFREUEN

The Postlude.....ʺAll Creatures of Our God and Kingʺ
. . . . arr.Young